ISBN: 9781290552356

Published by:
HardPress Publishing
8345 NW 66TH ST #2561
MIAMI FL 33166-2626

Email: info@hardpress.net
Web: http://www.hardpress.net

MORNING EXERCISES FOR ALL THE YEAR

MORNING EXERCISES

FOR ALL THE YEAR

A Day Book for Teachers

BY

JOSEPH C. SINDELAR

Author of NIXIE BUNNY IN MANNERS-LAND
NIXIE BUNNY IN WORKADAY-LAND
THE BEST CHRISTMAS BOOK

BECKLEY-CARDY COMPANY

CHICAGO

PREFACE

THIS book aims at a systematic and orderly presentation of the morning or opening exercise in the elementary school. Material is provided for every day of the school year, beginning with the first day in September and ending with the last day in June. There are as many exercises as there are days in the month, thus leaving the teacher free to a choice of lesson each day. If she feels that the psychological moment has arrived to consider a certain topic with her school she need not necessarily follow the subject outlined for that particular day.

It is the author's belief that the time has come for a more earnest consideration of moral training and that the teaching of morals can usually be accomplished more effectively through an indirect method than by set lessons or formal teaching. Character is largely a matter of habit and too great emphasis cannot be placed upon the early training in right attitude and right conduct. The choice of subjects should be more or less incidental. When certain events occur in the life of the nation or society which have ethical value, or when the birthdays of famous poets or statesmen or those of national heroes revive the memory of their virtues, the topic of the lesson is naturally determined thereby. Through concrete examples presented in story and verse the children learn to appreciate and admire nobility of character and deed and their best aspirations are thus aroused. But it is better to allow the child to make his own inference than to force the moral upon him.

The arrangement of this book, it is believed, will be found convenient and the plan novel. It is truly a day book for the teacher, correlating as it does, memory work, narrative, songs and music, birthday and holiday commemorations and those of the seasons, together with nature, literature, science and art.

Five lines of thought have been kept constantly in mind. First: The teaching of the common virtues through memory selections culled from the best in literature. There can be nothing better than the learning of these golden gems. Second: Through the story which is related to the quotation and the daily topic. Third: Through biography, using famous characters of history and literature to arouse ideals, to kindle ambition, and to nourish a belief in one's power to do something and' to cultivate a sense of worth and a feeling of self-respect. Fourth: Through the song, which conforms daily to the thought of the lesson. Fifth: Through the references which allow an enlarging upon the subject in hand. These consist of songs, additional stories and poems, Bible readings, birthdays and special days. It is well to speak of the birthday of an author or other noted person on the day before its occurrence and ask the pupils to be able to tell something of interest in regard to the person the next morning. In the case of an author pupils should be asked to bring in to be read or recited one or more selections from his works. In that of an artist, show reproductions of some of his paintings. In that of a musician have one or more of his compositions played or sung.

J. C. S.

CONTENTS

MORNING EXERCISES FOR ALL THE YEAR

SEPTEMBER

1 LABOR DAY

[Labor Day is the first Monday in September and is a legal holiday in nearly every state of the Union.]

> Work for some good, be it ever so slowly;
> Cherish some flower, be it ever so lowly;
> Labor, all labor is noble and holy.
> —*Mrs. F. S. Osgood*

LABOR DAY: ITS ORIGIN AND OBSERVANCE

LABOR DAY owes its origin to several causes. Perhaps the earliest of these was the formation of labor societies, such as the *Knights of Labor*, which was founded in Philadelphia in 1869. At one of the meetings of this society in New York City in 1882, a suggestion was offered that one day of the year be set aside when laborers or workingmen should not labor, but might go out and show that labor in this country is free and dignified. Later, some of the states passed laws making Labor Day a holiday, because the legislators wished to show their sympathy with the working class, many of whom could not afford to miss a day's pay by taking a vacation, and so a day was set apart when they could legally enjoy themselves and not lose their wages. In other states it was adopted for political reasons, the leaders hoping thus to secure the good will and the votes of the workingmen for whom they obtained the holiday.

The idea has been growing in favor since the first Labor Day, in 1888, when Colorado, Massachusetts, New Jersey and New York observed the day as a legal holiday. In 1894 Congress passed an act making the first Monday in September a legal public holiday, or "national holiday." This law is a recognition by the national government of the importance and significance of the new holiday, which had already been made a legal holiday in twenty-seven states and one territory.

Read: "Labor is Worship," by Frances S. Osgood; "The Man with the Hoe," by Edwin Markham; "Burden of Labor" and "The Village Blacksmith," by Henry W. Longfellow; "The Song of the Shirt," by Thomas Hood; Bible, Matt. 25: 14-30.

Sing: "Labor Day," from *Songs in Season.*

Birthday: Mrs. Lydia H. Sigourney, an American author, born in Norwich, Conn., September 1, 1791; died in Hartford, Conn., June 10, 1865.

2   THE CHILDREN'S POET

I look in the brook and see a face,
  Heigh-ho, but the years go by!
The rushes are dead in the old-time place,
  And the willows I knew when a child was I.
And the brook it seemeth to me to say,
As ever it stealeth on its way,
Solemnly now and not in play:
    "Oh, come with me
      To the slumberous sea
That is gray with the peace of the evening sky!"
  Heigh-ho, but the years go by,
  I would to God that a child were I!
                    —*Eugene Field*

THE STORY OF EUGENE FIELD

To-day is the birthday of one of the best friends that children ever had. Eugene Field was a little Western boy who lived with his aunt, his mother having died when he was but seven years old. His father did not live with him, but they corresponded regularly, so that Eugene learned early to express his thoughts in writing. He was of a rollicking, joyous disposition, and so made many friends at school. Later he went to college and studied law as his father had done. But law did not appeal to his poetic temperament and he soon gave that up so that he might devote all his time to writing.

He loved little children and would lay aside his work at any time to play with them, tell them stories, or sing them beautiful lullabies. He used to buy all sorts of queer toys, playthings, and sugar plums for his own little children and for little strangers with whom he always made friends. He knew that these are the things that children love best and we find his verses full of them. Mr. Field also loved flowers, beautiful pictures and animals. He always had pets about him and these he cared for himself with the greatest tenderness. He was devoted to his wife and home, and could never bear to be away from them for very long at a time. He had the most precious memory of his mother, and it often made him feel sad to think that she had so early in life been taken away from him. "I have a thousandfold more than my deserts," he would say, "yet, if my mother had but lived to feel a little, just a little, proud of her boy."

Read: "Wynken, Blynken, and Nod," the most perfect child poem ever written; "Little Boy Blue," "The Sugar-Plum Tree," "The Duel," "Sleepy Song." Chutter's *Art-Literature Third Reader* contains many stories and poems in the section devoted to Eugene Field.

Sing: Any of Field's beautiful lyrics set to music as found in *Songs of Childhood*.

Birthday: Eugene Field, "the children's poet," born in St. Louis, Mo., September 2, 1850; died in Chicago, Ill., November 4, 1895.

3 WORK

Let Labor, then look up and see
  His craft no pith of honor lacks;
The soldier's rifle yet shall be
  Less honored than the woodman's axe.

KINGS OF THE PAST AND PRESENT

THE kings of the past have sat on thrones and made others serve them. The kings of the future will be those who do the world's work and serve others best. We honor the man who works with his hands and conquers the earth. His hands may be coarse, his body bent, but if his work is honest, he is king as much as any man. We also honor the man who works with his brain. He who works honestly and well with his hands, blesses the world; he who works honestly and well with his brain, and gives to the world a good book, a noble picture, an inspiring song, labors to leave a blessing in the mind of another that will live when the things built with the hand alone have fallen to pieces.

Read: "The Sailor Man," from *The Pig Brother*, by Laura E. Richards; "For a' That," by Robert Burns; "Workingman's Song," by Charles Mackay; Bible, Prov. 6:6-11.

Sing: "Work, for the Night is Coming," from *Uncle Sam's School Songs*.

4 PERSEVERANCE

There are as many pleasant things,
  As many pleasant tones,
For those who dwell by cottage hearths
  As those who sit on thrones.
          —*Phœbe Cary*

THE STORY OF PHŒBE CARY

PHŒBE CARY was born in a low and small brown house, which stood on an old-fashioned country homestead or farm. Her mother died when Phœbe was a little girl, and as her father was poor, neither she nor her sister Alice could attend school very much. But they studied and read a great deal at home. As they had no lamps in the houses then, and her father couldn't afford candles, the two girls made a lamp by using a saucer with a rag in it for a wick, and by this strange light they would read and write until late into the night. When Phœbe was fourteen she began to compose verses, and at seventeen she was able to write quite well. She and her sister lived together all their lives and cared much for each other. The last twenty years of their lives were spent at their home in New York City, but they never forgot "the good old-fashioned homestead" where they were born. They both died the same year, in 1871.

Read: "Nobody's Child," "Our Homestead," "Suppose" and "Now," by Phœbe Cary; Mary Clemmer's *Memorial of Alice and Phœbe Cary,* and Whittier's "The Singer."

Sing: "Nearer Home" (a hymn by Phœbe Cary), found in almost any hymn book.

Birthday: Phœbe Cary, an American poet, born near Cincinnati, Ohio, September 4, 1824; died in Newport, R. I., July 31, 1871.

5 PATIENCE

Just a little every day;
    That's the way
Children learn to read and write,
Bit by bit and mite by mite,
    Never any one, I say,
Leaps to knowledge and its power.
Slowly, slowly—hour by hour—
    That's the way;
    Just a little every day.
        —*Ella Wheeler Wilcox*

6 PATRIOTISM

The moment I heard of America, I loved her; the moment I knew she was fighting for freedom, I burnt with a desire of bleeding for her; and the moment I shall be able to serve her at any time or in any part of the world, will be the happiest one of my life.

—*Lafayette*

AMERICA'S DEBT TO LAFAYETTE

AMERICA owes a great deal to this gallant young Frenchman[1] who crossed the seas to aid the colonies. He was among the first of those foreigners who showed the colonists that the love of liberty was as wide as the world. He came when hope was low, and his coming meant much to the brave men who had to undergo the long, discouraging winter at Valley Forge, and the days when it seemed as though time would prove them only rebels and not patriots. He brought ships, and men, and money to aid in the great cause, but more than all these were his own magnetic personality and the buoyant spirit that refused to be cast down.   —*Historic Boyhoods*

Read: "Lafayette, the Boy of Versailles," from *Historic Boyhoods*, by Holland; *Story of Lafayette*, by Margaret J. Codd.

Sing: "Hail! Columbia," from *American School Songs*.

Birthday: Marquis de Lafayette, born in Auvergne, France, September 6, 1757; died in Paris, France, May 20, 1834.

7 CHARITY

This world is not so bad a world
As some would like to make it:
Though whether good or whether bad,
Depends on how we take it.
—*M. W. Beck*

---

[1]He was but twenty years old then, having set sail for America April 20, 1777, in a boat happily named *La Victoire*.

THE DOVE AND THE WOODPECKER

A DOVE and a woodpecker had been visiting a peacock. "How did you like our host?" asked the woodpecker, after their visit. "Is he not very disagreeable! His vanity, shapeless feet, and his harsh voice are unbearable. Don't you think so?" "Indeed I had no time," said the gentle dove, "to notice these things; I was so occupied with the beauty of his head, the gorgeousness of his colors, and the majesty of his train."

Sing: "Life is What We Make It," from *Merry Melodies.*

8 AUTUMN

Summer's a step behind us,
   And Autumn's a thought before,
And each fleet, sweet day that we meet on the way
   Is an angel at the door.

Read: "The Anxious Leaf," from *Household Stories,* by Klingensmith.
"Autumn Leaves," from *Songs in Season.*
Sing: "Autumn," from *American School Songs,* or
Birthdays: Ludovico Ariosto, a famous Italian poet, born at Reggio, Italy, September 8, 1474; died in Ferrara, Italy, June 6, 1533.
Antonin Dvorak, a noted musician, born in Mühlhausen, Bohemia, September 8, 1841; died in Prague, Bohemia, May 1, 1904.

9 HABITS

How shall I a habit break?
As you did that habit make.
As we builded stone by stone,
We must toil unhelped, alone,
'Till the wall is overthrown.
                    —*O'Reilly*

THE FORMING OF HABITS

How are habits formed? When we repeat an act many times, we finally do it easily without thinking, and it becomes a habit. In time we find it difficult to do that thing in a different way, or to leave off doing it. Walking is a habit. So are sitting and standing in a certain way. There are two kinds of habits: good habits and bad habits. One's habits make up one's character. What are some of the good habits? Cleanliness, politeness, obedience, cheerfulness, good will, self-control, industry, courage, generosity, honesty, respect.) Bad habits? (Swearing, gossiping, drinking, smoking, etc.) Have you ever watched a monkey imitate the actions of a person? Have you ever "caught" the habits of another person, as biting the nails, talking or laughing loudly, shuffling or dragging the feet, squinting? Good habits make gentlemen and ladies of us. They also make many friends for us. Habits make or ruin our lives. Therefore, too great stress cannot be laid on the early forming of good habits.

10 HABITS
[Continued]

All habits gather by unseen degrees
As brooks make rivers, rivers run to seas.
—Dryden

HABIT

THERE was once a horse that used to pull around a sweep which lifted dirt from the depths of the earth. He was kept at the business for nearly twenty years, until he became old, blind and too stiff in the joints for further use. So he was turned into a pasture, or left to crop the grass without any one to disturb or bother him. But the funny thing about the old horse was that every morning after grazing awhile he would start on a tramp, going round and round in a circle, just as he had been accustomed to do for so many years. He would keep it up for hours, and people often stopped to look and wonder what had got into the head of the venerable animal to make him walk around in such a solemn way when there was no earthly need of it. But it was the force of habit. And the boy who forms bad or good habits in his youth will be led by them when he becomes old, and will be miserable or happy accordingly.

—*The Evangelist*

Sing: "Be Careful What You Sow," from *American School Songs.*

11 CONTENTMENT

Why sigh you for jewels? There's plenty, I ween,
For out on the currant-bush rubies I've seen.
There are emeralds hid in each glistening leaf,
And topazes rare in the wheat's golden sheaf;
There are pearls on the snow-berry bush, little lass,
And diamonds hid in the dew on the grass.
Then search in the garden, in morn's early dew;
Go gather your jewels, God made them for you.

—*A Little Maid's Jewels*

Read: "The Discontented Pine Tree," from *Household Stories,* by Klingensmith; "The Country Mouse and the Town Mouse," from Scudder's *Fables and Folk Stories;* "Cornelia's Jewels," from Baldwin's *Fifty Famous Stories Retold.*

12 TRUE WORTH

A great nation is made only by worthy citizens.
—*Charles Dudley Warner*

ROOM AT THE TOP

It is related of Mr. Webster that, when a young lawyer suggested to him that the profession to which he had devoted himself was overcrowded, the great man replied, "Young man, there is always room enough at the top."

Never was a wiser or more suggestive word said.   There undoubtedly is always room enough where excellency lives.
—*Josiah G. Holland*

Read: "He Aimed High and Hit the Mark" and "There is Room Enough at the Top," from Marden's *Stories from Life.*
Sing: "Learn a Little Every Day," from *Merry Melodies.*
Birthdays: Richard J. Gatling, the inventor of the Gatling gun, which is used in the United States army, born in Hertford Co., N. C., September 12, 1818; died in New York City, February 26, 1903.
Charles Dudley Warner, an American writer, born in Plainfield, Mass., September 12, 1829; died October 20, 1900.

13   SEPTEMBER DAYS

September days are here,
With summer's best of weather
And autumn's best of cheer.
—*Helen Hunt Jackson*

Sing: "September Days," from Hanson's *Gems of Song.*

14   OBEDIENCE

If you're told to do a thing,
And mean to do it really,
Never let it be by halves;
Do it fully, freely.
—*Phœbe Cary*

THE GIRL IN THE BROOK

One day Mary and her mother crossed the little stream that came from the pond. The stones and sand were white and smooth.

"May I play in the water, Mother?" asked Mary. "Yes, if you turn your dress up so that it will not get wet," said her mother.

By and by there was a noise like thunder. It seemed to come from the pond.

"Quick, Mary, come here," cried her mother. Mary did not stop to ask why. She ran to the place where her mother stood. Then she looked back. The stream was pouring over the rocks. The great water-gate by the dam was open. If Mary had waited she would have been carried down the stream into the river. There is not always time to ask why. —*N. Y. Teachers' Monographs*

Read: "Raggylug," as adapted from Ernest Thompson Seton's *Wild Animals I Have Known*, in *How to Tell Stories to Children*, by Sara Cone Bryant; Bible, Prov. 4: 1-5.

Sing: "Duty and Inclination," from *Uncle Sam's School Songs.*

Birthday: Charles Dana Gibson, an American artist, born in Roxbury, Mass., September 14, 1867; lives in New York City.

15 COURAGE

If you are about to strive for your life, take with you a stout heart and a clean conscience, and trust the rest to God.—*From "The Pilot," by J. Fenimore Cooper.*

COOPER'S LITERARY LIFE

COOPER's literary life is said to have begun in rather a curious way. One evening while reading an English novel to his wife, he declared that he could write a better one himself. To prove it he wrote *Precaution*, which was published anonymously in 1819. The book attracted very little attention and is said to have been disowned by its author. However, this did not discourage Cooper. In fact it set him to work harder than ever to prove his contention, and in 1821, *The Spy,* a novel founded on incidents of the American Revolution, was published and became popular at once. This was followed by thirty-eight other books, nearly all of which are widely read and liked.

Read: Selections from Cooper's works, as *The Deer-slayer, The Spy, The Pilot, The Last of the Mohicans,* etc.

Sing: "The Secret of Success," from *Uncle Sam's School Songs.*

Birthdays: James Fenimore Cooper, a noted American novelist, born at Burlington, N. J., September 15, 1789; died at Cooperstown, N. Y., September 14, 1851.

William Howard Taft, twenty-seventh President of the United States, born in Cincinnati, Ohio, September 15, 1857.

16 WORK

> Let us, then, be up and doing,
> With a heart for any fate;
> Still achieving, still pursuing,
> Learn to labor and to wait.
> —*Longfellow*

Birthdays: Anne Bradstreet, author of the first book of poetry written in America, born in Northampton, England, about 1612; died at Andover, Mass., September 16, 1672.

Francis Parkman, an American writer of history, born in Boston, Mass., September 16, 1823; died at Jamaica Plain, near Boston, November 8, 1893.

Hamlin Garland, an American author, born at West Salem, Wis., Sept. 16, 1861; lives in Chicago.

17 GRATITUDE

> I thank Thee, Lord, for quiet rest,
> And for Thy care of me;
> Oh, let me through this day be blest,
> And kept from harm by Thee.

Oh, let me thank Thee; kind Thou art
  To children such as I;
Give me a gentle, loving heart;
  Be Thou my Friend on high.

Help me to please my parents dear,
  And do whate'er they tell;
Bless all my friends, both far and near,
  And keep them safe and well.

—Osgood

18 PERSEVERANCE

Great works are performed, not by strength but by perseverance.—*Samuel Johnson*

THE STORY OF SAMUEL JOHNSON

WHEN Samuel Johnson was a little boy, his family was very poor, and his chances of obtaining an education were slight. His father was a bookseller, and as soon as little Samuel was old enough he would visit his father's shop and pore over the books on the shelves. Most boys would have learned little this way, but much that was dull to ordinary lads was interesting to Samuel.

While he was thus picking up knowledge, his father's business declined, and the family was placed in hopeless poverty. Samuel studied several years at Oxford, but was too poor to finish his course. He was being sneered at for his ragged appearance. Fun was made of him because of the holes in his shoes. Then his father died, after which for a good many years Samuel's life was one hard struggle with poverty.

He opened a school, but this proved a failure. He wasn't going to give up, however, and so began writing for magazines and doing other literary work for very small pay. Later he became famous as a writer. He prepared the first good dictionary of the English language that was ever written. One of his books is said to have been written in the evenings of a single week.

Birthday: Samuel Johnson, a famous English writer, born in Lichfield, England, September 18, 1709; died in London, England, December 13, 1784.

19 WORK

The heights by great men reached and kept
Were not attained by sudden flight;
But they, while their companions slept,
Were toiling upward through the night.
—Longfellow

Read: "I Will Paint or Die," and "The Boy Who Said 'I Must,'" from Marden's *Stories from Life;* Bible, Prov. 10:1-5.

Sing: "Work and Play," from Kellogg's *Best Primary Songs.*

20 TRUTHFULNESS

Oh, what a tangled web we weave
When first we practice to deceive.
—Scott

PRESIDENT GRANT'S WAY

A very important meeting was being held in the Capitol at Washington. A caller asked to see President Grant. Some one said to the servant who brought the message: "Tell the man that President Grant is not in."

"No," said the President, who heard the order, "tell him no such thing. I don't lie myself, and I don't wish any of my servants to lie for me."

Read: "George Washington and His Hatchet," from Baldwin's *Fifty Famous Stories;* "The Honest Woodman," from *Boston Collection of Kindergarten Stories.*

21 WRONGING OTHERS

Oh, many a shaft at random sent
Finds mark the archer little meant;
And many a word at random spoken,
May soothe or wound a heart that's broken.
—Scott

AN INCIDENT IN SCOTT'S LIFE

SIR WALTER SCOTT related the following incident of his own life to an intimate friend:

There was a boy in his class at school, who always stood at the top, nor could the utmost efforts of young Scott displace him. At length he observed, when a question was asked this boy, he always fumbled with his fingers at a particular button on the lower part of his waistcoat; and the removal of this was, therefore, determined. The plot was executed, and succeeded too well. When the boy was again questioned, his fingers sought again for the button, but it could not be found. In his distress he looked down for it, but it was not to be seen. He stood confounded, and Scott took possession of his place, which the boy never recovered. The wrong thus done was, however, attended, as it always must be, with pain. "Often," said Scott, "in after life, the sight of him smote me." Heartily did he wish that this unkind act had never been done.

Let it constantly be remembered, that we are not left to act as we please;—the rule is of the highest authority: *"Whatsoever ye would that men should do to you, do ye even so to them."*

Birthdays: Louis Joliet, a French traveler, one of the first to explore the Mississippi river, born in Quebec, Ontario, Canada, September 21, 1645; died in the year 1700.

John Loudon Macadam, inventor of the roads called after him "macadamized roads," born in Ayr, Scotland, September 21, 1756; died at Moffat, Scotland, November 26, 1836.

Sir Walter Scott, a famous Scottish novelist and poet, born in Edinburgh, Scotland, August 15, 1771; died at Abbotsford, Scotland, September 21, 1832.

22 POLITENESS

Hearts, like doors, will ope with ease
To very, very little keys;
And don't forget that two are these:
I thank you, sir, and *If you please.*

23 TRUE WORTH

Traverse the desert, and ye can tell
What treasures exist in the cold deep well;
Sink in despair on the red parch'd earth,
And then ye may reckon what water is worth.
—*Eliza Cook*

THE KING'S GARDEN

ONCE there was a king who owned a beautiful flower garden. One evening he walked among his flowers, glad that they were so full of beauty. The next morning one of his servants told him that his garden had been destroyed in the night.

The king hurried to the garden, and found the roses hanging their heads; the vines lying withered on the ground, and the trees quite leafless. Of one of the roses he asked: "Why is this?" The rose replied: "What is the use of blooming? A rose can live but a day or two at most." The king asked the same question of the vine. It answered: "It is so little that we can give. We had better give nothing." The tree said: "I am useless. I just stand here idle."

Then at his feet the king saw a little pansy blooming beautifully. He asked why it was not fading too, and it replied, "King, you put me here, and I try to be just the best little flower I can."

Then the king said: "O flowers, vine, and tree, if each one does his best, even though it be but little, what more can he do?"   —*Selected*

Sing: "Looks, Words and Deeds," from Kellogg's *Best Primary Songs.*

Birthday: Eliza Cook, an English poet, born in London, England, about 1818; died at Thornton Hall, Wimbledon, England, September 23, 1889.

24 KINDNESS TO ANIMALS

I will try to be kind to all harmless, living creatures, and to protect them from cruel usage.
—Pledge of Band of Mercy

LINCOLN'S KINDNESS TO BIRDS

THE following incident is related by one who knew Lincoln, and who, at the time of the incident, was his fellow-traveler.

We passed through a thicket of wild plum and crabapple trees, and stopped to water our horses. One of the party came up alone, and we inquired, "Where is Lincoln?"

"Oh," he replied, "when I saw him last, he had caught two young birds which the wind had blown out of their nest, and he was hunting for the nest that he might put them back in it."

In a short time Lincoln came up, having found the nest and restored the birds. The party laughed at his care of the young birds; but Lincoln said, "I could not have slept if I had not restored those little birds to their mother."

Read: "Androclus and the Lion," from Baldwin's *Fifty Famous Stories Retold.*

Sing: "The Bird with a Broken Wing," from *Uncle Sam's School Songs.*

Birthdays: Antoine Louis Barye, a famous sculptor, celebrated for his animal sculptures, born in Paris, France, September 24, 1795; died in Paris, June 25, 1875.

John Marshall, chief-justice of the United States, born in Fauquier Co., Va., September 24, 1755; died in Philadelphia, Pa., July 6, 1835.

25   CHARACTER

Oh! let us live, so that flower by flower,
   Shutting in turn may leave
A lingerer still for the sunset hour,
   A charm for the shaded eve.
          —*Mrs. Felicia D. Hemans*

Read: "The Point of View," from *The Golden Windows*, by Richards.

Sing: "To Our Friends," from Kellogg's *Best Primary Songs*.

Birthdays: Mrs. Felicia D. Hemans, an English poet, born in Liverpool, England, September 25, 1794; died near Dublin, Ireland, May 12, 1835.

Gaetano Donizetti, a noted Italian writer of operas, born in Bergamo, Italy, September 25, 1798; died in Bergamo, April 8, 1848. Composer of *La Favorita, Lucia di Lammermoor*, and about sixty other operas.

26   PATIENCE

Teach me, Father, how to be,
Kind and patient as a tree.
          —*Edwin Markham*

Read: "How the Leaves Came Down," by Susan Coolidge; "Talking in Their Sleep," by Edith Thomas; "The Little Rooster," from *Boston Collection of Kindergarten Stories*.

Sing: "Morning Song," from Hanson's *Gems of Song*.

27   NEATNESS

Let thy mind's sweetness have its operation
Upon thy body, clothes, and habitation.

THE BOY WHO RECOMMENDED HIMSELF

A GENTLEMAN advertised for a boy to assist him in his office, and nearly fifty applicants presented themselves to him. Out of the whole number, he selected one, and dismissed the rest. "I should like to know," said a friend, "on what ground you selected that boy, who had not a single recommendation." "You are mistaken," said the gentleman, "he had a great many. He wiped his feet when he came in, and closed the door after him, showing that he was careful. He gave his seat instantly to that lame old man, showing that he was kind and thoughtful. He took off his cap when he came in, and answered my questions promptly, showing that he was polite and gentlemanly. He picked up the book, which I had purposely laid on the floor, and replaced it upon the table, while all the rest stepped over it, showing that he was orderly; and he waited quietly for his turn, instead of pushing and crowding. When I talked to him, I noticed that his clothing was tidy, his hair neatly brushed, and his finger nails clean. Do you not call these things letters of recommendation? I do." —*Little Corporal*

Birthday: Samuel Adams, an American patriot and one of the signers of the Declaration of Independence, born in Boston, Mass., September 27, 1722; died in Boston, October 2, 1803.

28 CHARITY

I will speak more kindly and considerately to those whose claims are unrecognized by the society in which I live, than I will to others. I will bow more cordially to those to whom persons of position do not bow at all, and I will try in a thousand pleasant, nameless ways to make them happier. God help me to keep my promise good!—*Frances E. Willard*

Birthday: Frances E. Willard, lecturer, reformer and philanthropist, born in Churchville, N. Y., September 28, 1839; died in New York City, February 17, 1898.

29 TEMPERANCE

More are drowned in the bowl than in the sea.
—*Publius Syrus*

THE TWO WORKERS

BY JOHN W. AVERY

Two workers in one field
  Toiled on from day to day;
Both had the same hard labor,
  Both had the same small pay,
With the same blue sky above,
  And the same green earth below,
One soul was full of love,
  The other full of woe.

One leaped up with the light,
  With the soaring of the lark;
One felt his woe each night,
  For his soul was ever dark.
One heart was hard as stone,
  One heart was ever gay;
One toiled with many a groan,
  One whistled all the day.

One had a flower-clad cot
  Beside a merry mill;
Wife and children near the spot,
  Made it sweeter, fairer still. .
One a wretched hovel had,
  Full of discord, dirt and din;
No wonder he seemed mad,
  Wife and children starved within.

Still they worked in the same field,
  Toiling on from day to day;
Both had the same hard labor,
  Both had the same small pay.

But they worked not with one will—
The reason, let me tell:
Lo! one drank at the still,
And the other at the well.

Read: Bible, Prov. 20:1; 21:17; 23:19-23.
Sing: "The Flower's Drink," from *Uncle Sam's School Songs.*
Birthday: John McAllister Schofield, an American general, born in Chautauqua Co., N. Y., September 29, 1831; died March 4, 1906.

30 FIDELITY IN DUTY

Though your duty may be hard,
Look not on it as an ill;
If it be an honest task
Do it with an honest will.
—*Richard B. Sheridan*

THE FAITHFUL LITTLE HOLLANDER

IN SOME parts of Holland the land lies so low, that the people build great walls of earth, called dikes, to keep out the sea. Sometimes the waves break down these walls, and then the sea rushes in through the breach, and spreads over the land, often doing great damage. Houses have thus been washed away, and many people drowned.

Once as a little boy was going home in the evening, he saw a hole in one of the dikes, through which the water was trickling. His father had often told him that when this happened, unless the water was stopped, it would soon make the hole so large that the sea would rush in and overflow the land.

At first he thought he would run home and tell his father. But then he said to himself, "It may be dark before father can come, and we shall not be able to find the hole again; or it may get so large that it will be too late to stop it. I must stay now, and do the best I can alone."

The brave little boy sat down, and stopped the hole with earth, holding it with his hand to keep back the water. There he staid hour after hour in the cold and the dark, all through the night.

In the morning a man came past and saw him. He could not think what the boy was doing; and so he called out to him, "What are you doing there, my boy?"—"There is a hole in the dike," said the boy, "and I am keeping back the water."

Poor little boy! He was so cold and tired that he could scarcely speak. The man came quickly and set him free. He had the hole closed up, and thus the land was saved, thanks to the faithful and brave boy.   —*Royal Reader*

Read: "Findelkind," by De la Ramée, from *Bimbi Stories.*

Sing: "Here's to that Boy," from *Uncle Sam's School Songs.*

Birthday: Richard B. Sheridan, a British writer and statesman, born in Dublin, Ireland. September 30, 1751; died in London, England, July 7, 1816.

OCTOBER

1 HEROISM

Heroism is simple, and yet it is rare. Every one who does the best he can is a hero.—Josh Billings

"DON'T GIVE UP THE SHIP!"

In the War of 1812, there was in our navy a ship called the *Hornet,* with Captain James Lawrence as its commander. One day it engaged in battle with the English vessel *Peacock.* So fast and so thick flew the balls, so hot and so terrible was the battle, that in fifteen minutes the proud Peacock had lost all her glory and her pride, all her beauty and her courage, and lay upon the waters a complete wreck. Her commander surrendered to Lawrence, the crew were taken prisoners and transferred to the Hornet.

Later Captain Lawrence was given another vessel and met the English vessel *Shannon* in battle. After a hot, fierce battle Lawrence's ship was wrecked and Lawrence himself, who always stood in the very thickest of the fire, was mortally wounded.

Very carefully did his officers carry below their much loved commander; and Lawrence, not forgetting his charge even in dying, whispered, almost with his last breath, "Don't give up the ship!"   —*Adapted*

Sing: "America" or "The Star-Spangled Banner."

Birthday: James Lawrence, a noted American naval officer, born in Burlington, N. J., October 1, 1781; died January 5, 1813.

2 OCTOBER'S BRIGHT WEATHER

O suns and skies and flowers of June,
　　Count all your boasts together,
Love loveth best of all the year,
　　October's bright blue weather.
　　　　　—*Helen Hunt Jackson*

Birthday: Major John André, a British officer hanged as a spy in the War of the Revolution, born of Swiss parents in London, England, 1751; hanged at Tappan, N. Y., October 2, 1780.

3 FRIENDSHIP

The friendship between me and you I will not compare to a chain; for that rains might rust, or the falling tree might break.
　　　　　—*From "History of the United States,"*
　　　　　by George Bancroft

DAMON AND PYTHIAS

MORE than two thousand years ago two young men who were intimate friends lived in Greece. Their names were Damon and Pythias.

The ruler of the country, named Dionysius, was a cruel man. He put Pythias into prison and set a day for his death. Pythias had done nothing wrong, but he had convicted the ruler of wrong-doing.

The father and mother of Pythias lived in another part of the country. "May I go home to bid them good-by, and to arrange my affairs before I die?" he asked.

The ruler laughed. "That is a strange request," said he. "Of course you would escape and you would never come back."

At that moment Damon stepped forward. "I am his friend," he said. I will stay in prison till Pythias returns."

Then the ruler asked: "What will happen if Pythias does not return?"

"I will die for him," said Damon.

This surprised Dionysius very much. He put Damon in prison and Pythias went home. Weeks went by and Pythias did not return. At last the day of execution came, and Damon was led out to be put to death. He said: "Pythias will come if he is alive. I can trust him absolutely."

Just then soldiers ran up, shouting: "Here he comes! Here he comes!"

Yes, there was Pythias, breathless with haste. He had been shipwrecked on his journey and had been cast on shore many miles away. He had walked all those miles to get back in time.

Dionysius was greatly moved. "You are both free," said he. "I would give all I have for one such friend. Will you let me become a friend to you both?"

—*Ethics for Children*

Read: Bible, Prov. 27: 9-10.

Sing: "Auld Lang Syne."

Birthdays: Miles Standish, the first military leader of the Puritan settlers in New England, born in Lancashire, England, about 1584; died in Duxbury, Mass., October 3, 1656.

George Bancroft, an American statesman and historian, born in Worcester, Mass., October 3, 1800; died at Washington, D. C., January 17, 1891.

Elias Howe, a noted American inventor, born in Spencer, Mass., July 9, 1819; died in Brooklyn, N. Y., October 3, 1867.

4 HONOR

The soul asks honor, and not fame; to be upright, not to be successful, to be good, not prosperous; to be essentially, not outwardly, respectable.

—*Robert Louis Stevenson*

Birthdays: Jean Francois Millet, a French painter,

born in Gruchy, France, October 4, 1814; died at Barbizon, near Paris, France, January 18, 1875.

Rutherford B. Hayes, nineteenth president of the United States, born in Delaware, Ohio, October 4, 1822; died at Fremont, Ohio, January 17, 1893.

Frederic Remington, an American artist and author, born in Canton, N. Y., October 4, 1861; died at Ridgefield, Conn., December 26, 1909.

5 SELF-RELIANCE

I hold it truth with him who sings
To one clear harp in divers tones,
That men may rise on stepping-stones
Of their dead selves to higher things.
—*Tennyson*

THE JUDGE'S BENCH

One who cultivates self-reliance will grow stronger physically, mentally and morally. It is better for one to inherit a character for honesty, industry, and self-reliance than to inherit a fortune in money. The former may grow, the latter may go.

A former United States judge began his career as a carpenter, using his spare time in the study of law. One day he was planing a board which was to become a part of a judge's bench. A friend who was observing his pains-taking effort, said to him: "Why do you take so great pains to make it smooth?"

"Because I want a smooth seat when I come to sit upon it," was the reply. After a number of years of persistent effort he came to sit on that same bench.

Read: "The Lark and Her Young Ones," from *Boston Collection of Kindergarten Stories*.

Sing: "Life is Real, Life is Earnest," from *Uncle Sam's School Songs*.

Birthdays: Chester A. Arthur, twenty-first president of

the United States, born at Fairfield, Vt., October 5, 1830; died at New York City, November 18, 1886.

William Hamilton Gibson, American author, artist, and naturalist, born at Sandy Hook, Conn., October 5, 1850; died in Washington, Conn., July 16, 1896.

6 KINDNESS

Howe'er it be, it seems to me,
'Tis only noble to be good;
Kind hearts are more than coronets
And simple faith than Norman blood.
—*Tennyson*

Read: Selections from Tennyson's poems.

Sing: "Sweet and Low," from *Songs Every One Should Know;* "The Bugle Song," from Hanson's *Gems of Song.*

Birthdays: Alfred Lord Tennyson, a famous English poet, born at Somersby, Lincolnshire, England, August 6, 1809; died at Aldworth House, near Haslemere, Surrey, England, October 6, 1892.

Jenny Lind, a famous Swedish singer, born in Stockholm, Sweden, October 6, 1821; died November 2, 1887.

George Westinghouse, an American inventor and manufacturer, born at Central Bridge, Schoharie Co., N. Y., October 6, 1846; died in Pittsburgh, Pa., March 12, 1914.

7 HEALTH DAY

You hear that boy laughing? You think he's all fun,
But the angels laugh, too, at the good he has done;
The children laugh loud as they troop to his call,
And the poor man that knows him laughs loudest of all.
—*O. W. Holmes*

A HEALTH CREED

[For daily recitation]

To BE well I must keep my body, my clothes and my house clean.

I must have plenty of fresh air and of sunshine.

I must eat good food and chew it slowly and brush my teeth often.

I should drink plenty of water.

I must sit straight and stand straight, so as to breathe deep and grow up straight and strong.

Early to bed and a long night's sleep will rest my mind and body and keep me from being nervous.

—Alice C. Ryan

Birthday: Oliver Wendell Holmes, a noted American author, born in Cambridge, Mass., August 29, 1809; died in Boston, Mass., October 7, 1894.

8 GOOD DEEDS

> The words which thou hast uttered,
>   Are of thy soul a part.
> And the good seed thou hast scattered
>   Is springing from the heart.
>
> —Whittier

KINDNESS RETURNED

ONE day a lady who was riding in a stagecoach saw a lad on the road barefoot and seemingly very footsore. She asked the coachman to take him up, and said she would pay for him. When the coach reached the end of its journey, the kind lady found that the poor lad was bound for the nearest seaport, to offer himself as a sailor.

Twenty years afterwards, on the same road, a sea captain, riding on a stagecoach, saw an old lady walking wearily along, and he asked the coachman to pull up his horses. He then put the old lady inside the coach, saying, "I'll pay for her." When they next changed horses, the old lady thanked the captain, saying, "I am too poor to pay for a ride now."

The captain told her that he always felt for those who had to walk, as she had been doing, and added, "I remem-

ber, twenty years ago, near this very place, I was a poor
lad walking along the road, and a kind lady paid for me
to ride.''

''Ah!'' said she, ''I am that lady; but things have
changed with me since then.''

''Well,'' said the captain, ''I have made a fortune, and
have come home to enjoy it. I will allow you twenty-five
pounds a year as long as you live.'' The old lady burst
into tears, as she gratefully accepted the sailor's offer.

—White's School Management

Read: ''The Knights and the Good Child,'' from Bakewell's *True Fairy Stories.*

Birthdays: Rembrandt [Van Ryn], a famous Dutch
painter, born in Leyden, Netherlands, July 15, 1607; died
in Amsterdam, Netherlands, October 8, 1669.

Edmund Clarence Stedman, an American poet and critic,
born in Hartford, Conn., October 8, 1833; died at New
York City, January 18, 1908.

John Hay, an American author and diplomatist, born
at Salem, Ill., October 8, 1839; died at Newburg, N. H.,
July 1, 1905.

9 HAPPINESS

> The sweetest bird builds near the ground,
> The loveliest flowers spring low,
> And we must stoop for happiness
> If we its worth would know.
>
> —Swain

Read: ''The Miller of the Dee,'' from Baldwin's *Fifty
Famous Stories.*

Sing: ''Come with Thy Lute,'' from Kellogg's *Best
Primary Songs.*

Birthdays: Miguel de Cervantes Saavedra, a noted
Spanish writer, born at Alcala de Henares, Spain, October
9, 1547; died April 23, 1616, on the same day with Shakespeare. Author of *Don Quixote.*

Guiseppe Verdi, an Italian writer of music, born in the duchy of Parma, Italy, October 9 1814; died in Milan, Italy, January 26, 1901.

Leonard Wood, an American soldier, born at Winchester, N. H., October 9, 1860; at present, chief of staff of the army, living at Washington, D. C.

Harriet G. Hosmer, an American sculptor, born in Watertown, Mass., October 9, 1830.

10 CONSCIENCE

Do what conscience says is right;
Do what reason says is best;
Do with all your mind and might;
Do *your duty* and be blest.

LINCOLN'S CONSCIENTIOUSNESS

ABRAHAM LINCOLN held the office of postmaster at New Salem, Illinois, for three years. Several years later when he was a practicing lawyer, an agent called upon him, and asked for a balance of seventeen dollars due the government. Lincoln arose and opening a little trunk which lay in a corner of the room, took out from it a cotton rag in which was tied up the exact sum required. "I never use any man's money, but my own." he quietly remarked.

When we consider the poverty of those years, we can appreciate the self-denial that had kept him from making even a temporary use of that government money.

Sing: "Woodman, Spare That Tree," from *Songs Every One Should Know.*

Birthdays: George P. Morris, a noted American song writer, born in Philadelphia, Pa., October 10, 1802; died in New York City, July 6, 1864. Author of "Woodman, Spare That Tree," "My Mother's Bible," etc.

Mihaly Munkacsy, a Hungarian painter, born at Munkacs, Hungary, October 10, 1846; died in Bonn, Germany, May 1, 1900.

11 GOOD MANNERS

Good boys and girls should never say,
"I will," and "Give me these."
Oh, no, that never is the way,
But "Mother, if you please."

THE DRUM AND THE VASE OF SWEET HERBS

A DRUM was once boasting to a vase of sweet herbs in this way: "Listen to me! My voice is loud and can be heard far off. I stir the hearts of men so that when they hear my bold roaring they march out bravely to battle."

The vase spoke no words, but gave out a fine, sweet perfume that filled the air, and seemed to say: I cannot speak, and it is not well to be proud, but I am full of good things that are hidden within me, and that gladly come forth to give cheer and comfort. But you, you have nothing in you but noise, and you must be struck to make you give that out. I would not boast if I were you.

—Æsop

Read: "Please," by Alicia Aspinwall, in *Can You Believe Me Stories*.

Sing: "Kind Words," from Kellogg's *Best Primary Songs*.

12 COLUMBUS OR DISCOVERY DAY

Endurance is the crowning quality,
And patience all the passion of great hearts.
—From "Columbus," by Lowell

A LESSON IN COURAGE AND PERSEVERANCE

WASHINGTON IRVING in his *Life of Columbus* relates the following incident, which illustrates but one of the many great disappointments of the navigator.

While Columbus, his pilot, and several of his experienced mariners were studying the map, and endeavoring to make out from it their actual position, they heard a shout from the Pinta, and looking up, beheld Martin Alonzo Pinzon mounted on the stern of his vessel crying, "Land! land! Senor, I claim my reward!" He pointed at the same time to the southwest, where there was indeed an appearance of land at about twenty-five leagues' distance.

Upon this Columbus threw himself on his knees and returned thanks to God; and Martin Alonzo repeated the *Gloria in excelsis,* in which he was joined by his own crew and that of the admiral. The seamen now mounted to the masthead or climbed about the rigging, straining their eyes in the direction pointed out. The morning light, however, put an end to all their hopes, as to a dream. The fancied land proved to be nothing but an evening cloud, and had vanished in the night.

It is not certain, however, that the disappointments of to-day will not give place to realized hope to-morrow. Columbus was not discouraged; in fact nothing could turn him back, and hope had its final reward.

Read: James Russell Lowell's "Columbus," and Joaquin Miller's "Columbus."

Sing: "Columbus," from *Songs in Season.*

Birthdays: Christopher Columbus, the discoverer of the New World, born in or near Genoa, Italy, about 1446; died in Vallodolid, Spain, May 20, 1506.

Josiah G. Holland, an American writer, born in Belchertown, Mass., July 24, 1819; died in New York City, October 12, 1881.

Dinah Maria Mulock Craik [Miss Mulock], an English writer of novels and stories, born in Stoke-upon-Trent, England, in 1826; died at Shortlands, Kent, England, October 12, 1887.

Special Days: Anniversary of the discovery of America [Columbus Day]. Arbor Day in North Carolina. (See *Arbor Day,* April 19 and 20, this book.)

13 OPPORTUNITY

Do not cry and weep for chances,
Chances that have passed away,
Opportunities neglected—
Grasp the chance you have to-day.
—Selected

Read: "Day," by Richards, from *The Golden Windows.*
Sing: "The Jolly Workers," from Kellogg's *Best Primary Songs.*

14 JUSTICE

If those who've wronged us own their faults and kindly pity pray,
When shall we listen and forgive? To-day, my love, to-day.
But if stern justice urge rebuke, and warmth from memory borrow,
When shall we chide if chide we must? To-morrow, love, to-morrow.

WILLIAM PENN AND THE INDIANS

SOME of the early settlers of this country bargained with the Indians that for each fish-hook given, they were to give as much land as a bullock's hide would cover. But the settlers cut the hide into thin strips, and made it cover a large area. William Penn, when he first came to America, to Pennsylvania, bargained with the Indians that he would give a certain number of articles for as much land as a man could walk around in a certain time. The man covered so much more land than the Indians believed he would, that they became dissatisfied and threatening. But Penn said to them, "You agreed to this way of measuring." His companions wished to force the carrying out of this argument. But Penn replied that that would be wrong toward these simple children of the prairie; he asked them what they thought would be right, and they simply demanded a few more rolls of cloth, to which Penn agreed. Not only was war averted, but the Indians were pleased with the fair and just spirit shown by the strangers, and became their friends.   —*Popular Educator*

Read: Bible, Matt. 5: 38-48.

Birthday: William Penn, the founder of Pennsylvania, born in London, England, October 14, 1644; died at Ruscombe, Berkshire, England, July 30, 1718.

15   A SCHOOLROOM LESSON

If you've any task to do,
Let me whisper, friend, to you,
  Do it.

TURNING ABOUT

BY MARY J. MYERS

'Tis tempting sore, there is no doubt,
While at your desk, to turn about.
Your eyes you turn, your nose you point,
Your neck is sadly out of joint.

While turning round to look behind,
You miss what is before, you'll find,
And what's before is much worth while,
And looking forward's better style.

How very strange it all would be
If eyes were placed behind to see,
While mouth and chin and also toes
Were pointing forward with your nose.

So forward turn and danger spare,
And of your eyes and neck take care,
Lest kink in neck or eye refrain
From ever turning straight again.

Sing: "Opening Song," from *Uncle Sam's School Songs.*

16 WATCH YOUR WORDS

Keep a watch on your words, my darling,
  For words are wonderful things;
They are sweet like the bees' fresh honey—
  Like the bees they have terrible stings;
They can bless like the warm, glad sunshine,
  And brighten a lonely life,
They can cut, in the strife of anger,
  Like an open, two-edged knife.
                              —*Mrs. E. R. Miller*

Birthdays: Noah Webster, an American author, born in Hartford, Conn., October 16, 1758; died in New Haven, Conn., May 28, 1843.

Horace E. Scudder, an American writer, born in Boston, Mass., October 16, 1838; died in Cambridge, Mass., January 11, 1902.

17 OBEDIENCE

He who has learned to obey, will know how to command.
                              —*Solon*

A LESSON IN OBEDIENCE

ONE day General Washington, sending a dispatch, directed the bearer to cross the river at a certain ferry, and go through the Ramapo Pass to Morristown. The young man, knowing that a nest of traitors infested the pass, ventured to suggest to the Commander-in-chief that another road would be safer. "I shall be taken," he said, "if I go through the pass." "Young man, *your duty is not to talk, but to obey*," said Washington, sternly. He went as directed, and near the pass was captured, as he was afraid of being, and sent to New York, then in the hands of the enemy. The next day, the dispatches taken from him, disclosing a plan of attacking the city, were published with great parade, and the English immediately began preparations to defend it.

This gave Washington time to plan and execute *another*

movement in quite a different direction, and by that time both the British and the bearer found out that the dispatch was meant to be taken.

Read: "Bessie's Garden," from Whittier's *Child Life in Prose;* "Casabianca," from Baldwin's *Fifty Famous Stories Retold;* Bible, Prov. 3:1-7.

Sing: "How Happy is the Child," from *Kellogg's Best Primary Songs.*

18 PATIENCE

One day at a time. It's a wholesome rhyme;
A good one to live by, a day at a time.
            —*Helen Hunt Jackson*

Read: "October's Bright Blue Weather," by Helen Hunt Jackson; also sketch of her life, from *October Primary Plan Book.*

Sing: "There's Music in the Air," from *Uncle Sam's School Songs.*

Birthdays: Helen Hunt Jackson, an American writer, born at Amherst, Mass., October 18, 1831; died in San Francisco, Cal., August 12, 1885.

Thomas B. Reed, an American statesman, born in Portland, Me., October 18, 1839; died in Washington, D. C., September 7, 1902.

19 DEVOTION TO DUTY

Heaven is not reached at a single bound,
But we build the ladder by which we rise
From the lowly earth to the vaulted skies,
And we mount to its summit round by round.
            —*Holland*

THE LITTLE DRUMMER BOY

ONCE while in camp Napoleon Bonaparte stayed in a building with some soldiers, among whom he observed a little drummer boy, not yet twelve years of age. Calling the boy to him, the great Emperor asked, "My little man, what are you doing here?"

"I belong to the army, sire," replied the boy.

"What do you do in the army?" asked Napoleon.

"I am a drummer, sire," was the reply.

"Fetch your drum," said Napoleon. The drum was fetched and Napoleon said: "Sound the 'general' for me." Promptly the "general" was sounded by the little drummer, and the Emperor exclaimed, "Good! now, beat the 'march;'" and the boy obeyed. "Now, sound the 'advance,'" said Bonaparte, and with sparkling eyes the little Drummer sounded the "advance" in a firm, even measure. "Good!" exclaimed the Emperor, "Now for the 'charge'!" and with eyes flashing fire the little soldier beat the "charge" till the very rafters trembled from the vibrations of the wild, fierce notes. "Bravo!" cried Napoleon, "now beat for me the 'retreat.'" Down went the sticks. The little fellow straightened up and with a flush of manly pride, he said, "You must excuse me, sire, I never learned that. Our regiment never retreated." The great commander excused him, and it is said that even on St. Helena he often spoke of his little drummer boy who could not beat a "retreat."

Birthday: Edward Winslow, governor of Plymouth colony, born at Droitwich, Worcestershire, England, October 19, 1595; died at sea, May 8, 1655.

20 HUMILITY

Knowledge is proud that he has learned so much,
Wisdom is humble that he knows no more.
                                        —Cowper

SELF-PRAISE

A MAN once walked along the banks of the mighty Euphrates River. Its waters moved softly and silently

along. "Why do not thy waters surge and roar?" asked
the man. And the river replied: "I need not shout aloud;
my name is known widely enough. The green meadows
which I water and the lofty trees upon my banks—these
tell who I am."

The man came afterward to the banks of the Tigris
River. Its waves dashed along wildly and with clouds of
foam. "Hello, how loud you are shouting!" said the man.
"Ah," said the river, "my shouting does not help me at
all! I still am not praised like other streams, however
loudly I proclaim that I am something in the world."

The man went further. He saw trees with the costliest
and most beautiful fruit. They offered their fruits without a sound. "Why so still, good trees?" he asked. "Why
not rustle like your companions in the wood?" "We are
known," they replied, "by the fruit we bear, however
silent we are." Soon the man came to a wood whose trees
towered to the skies, and whose empty crests kept up a
constant roar. "Why do you make such a noise?" he
asked. "Ah," they replied, "we have shouted loud and
long, and yet we are not treated as we deserve."

"Now I know," said the man, "who praises himself
amounts to nothing. The truly meritorious require no self-
praise. That truth I will not forget."

—*Jewish Messenger*

Read: "The Fantail Pigeon," from Poulsson's *In the
Child's World.*

Sing: "Don't Talk When You've Nothing to Say,"
from *American School Songs.*

Birthdays: Henry Inman, an American painter, born in
Utica, N. Y., October 20, 1801; died in New York City,
January 17, 1846.

Thomas Hughes, an English author, born in Uffington,
Berkshire, England, October 20, 1823; died March 22,
1896.

21 MUSIC IN ALL THINGS

There's music in the sighing of a reed;
There's music in the gushing of a rill;
There's music in all things, if men had ears:
This earth is but an echo of the spheres.
—*Byron*

"AMERICA"

THIS most popular and best loved of all our national songs was written by Dr. Samuel F. Smith. One of Dr. Smith's best friends was Lowell Mason, the eminent musician. A German friend had given to Mr. Mason a number of German music books. Being unable to read German, Mr. Mason carried the books to Dr. Smith and asked him to translate some of the songs for him. What followed we will let Dr. Smith relate. He says: "Turning over the leaves of one of these books one day in February, 1832, I came across the air 'God Save the King.' I liked the music. I glanced at the German words at the foot of the page. Under the inspiration of the moment I went to work and in half an hour 'America' was the result. It was written on a scrap of paper I picked up from the table, and the hymn of to-day is substantially as it was written that day."

This hymn was first sung at a children's Fourth of July celebration in Park Street Church, Boston. It did not have great popularity until the Civil War. Since then it has become the best known of any of our national songs.

An incident in connection with the singing of "America," on one particular occasion, may be related here with profit. Not many years ago there was gathered in a United States consulate in a foreign land a few score Americans. It was the Fourth of July and the little band seemed particularly impressed with the significance of the day and the occasion. One member of the party suggested that they sing "America." He began the song, all sang the first stanza, a few sang the second, four voices blended together to the end of the third, and a single voice continued to the end. Only one person of all those gathered together knew his national song to the end. Is not this a lesson to us?

Sing: "America."

Birthdays: Samuel Taylor Coleridge, a noted English poet, born at Ottery Saint Mary, Devonshire, England, October 21, 1772; died in London. July 25, 1834.

Will Carleton, an American poet, born at Hudson, Mich., October 21, 1845. Editor of *Everywhere.*

Samuel F. Smith, an American clergyman, born in Boston, Mass., October 21, 1808; died in Boston, November 16, 1895. Author of song "America."

22 EVIL SPEAKING

Boys flying kites haul in their white-winged birds;
You can't do that way when you're flying words.
"Careful with fire," is good advice, we know;
"Careful with words," is ten times doubly so.
Thoughts unexpressed may sometimes fall back dead;
But God himself can't kill them when they're said.
—*Will Carleton*

THE SLANDERER

A LADY visited Sir Philip Neri on one occasion, accusing herself of being a slanderer.

"Do you frequently fall into this fault?" he inquired.

"Yes, very often," replied the penitent.

"My dear child," said Philip, "your fault is great, but the mercy of God is greater. I now bid thee do as follows: Go to the nearest market and purchase a chicken just killed and still covered with feathers; then walk to a certain distance, plucking the bird as you go. Your walk finished, return to me."

The woman did as directed and returned, anxious to know the meaning of so singular an injunction.

"You have been very faithful to the first part of my orders," said Philip; "now do the second part, and you will be cured. Retrace your steps, pass through all the places you have traversed, and gather up one by one all the feathers you have scattered."

"But," said the woman, "I cast the feathers carelessly away, and the wind carried them in all directions."

"Well, my child," replied Philip, "so it is with your words of slander. Like the feathers which the wind has scattered, they have been wafted in many directions: call them back now if you can. Go, sin no more."

Birthdays: Franz Liszt, a famous Hungarian pianist and composer of music, born at Raiding, October 22, 1811; died at Bayreuth, Bavaria, July 31, 1886.

Sarah Bernhardt, a celebrated French actress, born in Paris, France, October 22, 1844. (Her real name is Rosine Bernard.)

23 BEAUTIFUL THINGS

Beautiful faces are they that wear
The light of a pleasant spirit there;
It matters little if dark or fair.

Beautiful hands are they that do
Deeds that are noble, good and true;
Busy with them the long day through.

Beautiful feet are they that go
Swiftly to lighten another's woe,
Through the summer's heat or winter's snow.

Beautiful children, if, rich or poor,
They walk the pathways sweet and pure
That lead to the mansion strong and sure.
—*Mrs. E. R. Miller*

Sing: "Away with Melancholy," from *Uncle Sam's School Songs.*

Birthday: Francis Hopkinson Smith, an American

author, painter and civil engineer, born in Baltimore, Md., October 23, 1838; lives in New York City.

24 PURPOSE

I live for those who love me,
　　Whose hearts are fond and true.
For the heaven that smiles above me,
　　And awaits my spirit too;
For all human ties that bind me,
For the task by God assigned me,
For the bright hopes left behind me,
　　And the good that I can do.
　　　　　　　—*G. L. Banks*

THE TWO ROADS

BY JEAN PAUL RICHTER

IT WAS New Year's night. An aged man was standing at a window. He raised his mournful eyes toward the deep blue sky, where the stars were floating. like white lilies, on the surface of a clear, calm lake. Then he cast them down hopelessly on the earth.

Already he had passed sixty years of life, and he had brought from his journey nothing but errors and remorse. His health was destroyed. his mind vacant, his heart sorrowful, and his old age devoid of comfort.

The days of his youth rose up, in a vision, before him, and he recalled the solemn moment, when his father had placed him at the entrance of two roads,—*one* leading into a peaceful, sunny land, covered with a fertile harvest, and resounding with soft, sweet songs; while the *other* conducted the wanderer into a deep, dark cave, whence there was no issue, where poison flowed, instead of water, and where serpents hissed and crawled.

He looked toward the sky, and cried out in his agony: "O youth, return! O my father, place me once more at the entrance to life, that I may choose the better way!"

But the days of his youth and his father had both passed away.

Ye who still linger on the threshold of life, doubting which path to choose, remember that when years are passed, and your feet stumble on the dark mountain, you will cry bitterly, but cry in vain: *"O youth return! O, give me back my early days!"*   —*Adapted*

25 HONESTY

Thou must be true thyself,
If thou the truth wouldst teach;
Thy soul must overflow, if thou
Another's soul wouldst reach!
It needs the overflow of heart
To give the lips full speech.

Think truly, and thy thoughts
Shall the world's famine feed;
Speak truly, and each word of thine
Shall be a fruitful seed;
Live truly, and thy life shall be
A great and noble creed.
                —*Horatius Bonar*

Read: "The Honest Woodman," from *Boston Collection of Kindergarten Stories;* Bible, Prov. 22:1; Eccl. 7:1.

Sing: "Home, Sweet Home," from *Uncle Sam's School Songs.*

Birthdays: Geoffrey Chaucer, a famous English poet, born in London, England, about 1328; died in London, October 25, 1400. Author of the *Canterbury Tales.*

Thomas Babington Macaulay, a famous English historian, born in Leicestershire, England, October 25, 1800; died at Holly Lodge, Campden Hill, England, December 28, 1859.

26 THE RED CROSS

God be thanked that the dead have left still
Good undone for the living to do.
                —*Owen Meredith*

THE STORY OF THE RED CROSS FLAG

On Christmas Day, 1822, Clara Barton was born. As a child Miss Barton was painfully shy in the presence of strangers, so her parents finally decided to send her to boarding school, thus hoping to overcome this sensitiveness. Here her suffering was so acute that she was finally brought back home. What was to be done with her? The question solved itself. Her beloved brother David fell ill; the baby sister became his nurse, taking all the responsibility of his care upon herself; for two years she devoted herself to him. She thus forgot herself, and in a great measure conquered the shyness, which had made life a burden.

Next Miss Barton was a teacher, and then she became a clerk in the Patent Office in Washington. Soon began to be heard the rumblings of war, and then the rumbling became a mighty thundering and the Civil War was on. A regiment from Clara Barton's old home in Massachusetts was passing through Washington. Without consulting anyone, Clara Barton joined it, and so began her labor of love as an army nurse. Her clear insight, strong will, ability to do and direct work made her invaluable to the regiment. She became the natural leader in the work of relief. For four years Miss Barton followed the vicissitudes of a terrible warfare.

The Civil War closed, the army was disbanded, the soldiers went home. Not so Clara Barton; her work was not yet ended. Four additional years were given to organizing and carrying on a work of identifying the dead and delivering the messages of the dead and dying. Many a mother had cause to bless the name of Clara Barton, who sought her out to deliver the dying message of a beloved son.

Then came the Franco-Prussian war. All Europe was stirred. Clara Barton was visited by a band of people who were going to the center of the battle to help care for the sufferers. These people were organized for the work and had an organization behind them—it was the International Red Cross of Geneva. The object in having such an organization was that it should be recognized and respected on any battlefield anywhere. It was called the Red Cross— their emblem or flag was a Greek Cross in red on a white field. Thirty-one governments had signed this treaty; the United States had not. Clara Barton went to Europe, she nursed the soldiers through the Franco-Prussian war. She returned home. She realized that wherever there was war in the future that there the Red Cross must be found; she knew that the Red Cross was a benefit to humanity. She felt that the United States must sign this convention.

She determined to work to bring this about. She sought the officials at Washington, and told them the benefits to be derived from the Red Cross; she told them its history on these European battlefields; she was so earnest in her desire to aid her country that she won her cause. In the year 1882 the United States ratified this convention, and so we secured the protection of the Red Cross. Clara Barton was made the first president of the American National Red Cross Society. She made an able commander. She went, or sent relief corps and provisions to the Johnstown Flood, Russian Famine, South Carolina Tidal Wave, Armenian Massacre, and the Spanish-American war. Miss Barton died in 1912, at the age of ninety years.

Read: "The Red Cross," from Baldwin's *American Book of Golden Deeds;* "St. Elizabeth and the Sick Child," from Wiltse's *Kindergarten Stories and Morning Talks;* Bible, Matt. 5:6; Matt. 20:26-27.

Sing: "Flow Gently, Sweet Afton," from Hanson's *Gems of Song.*

Special Day: Anniversary of the origin of the Red Cross Society; emblem: red cross. Clara Barton was the founder of the Red Cross Society in America.

27 PERSEVERANCE

It is hard to fail, but it is worse never to have tried to succeed.—Theodore Roosevelt

ROBERT BRUCE AND THE SPIDER

IT WAS the perseverance of the spider that taught King Robert Bruce of Scotland the lesson that gained the victory at Bannockburn, the battle that made Scotland free. The King was out in a barn one day reconnoitering the army. While there reclining on the straw he saw a spider climbing up one of the rafters. The insect fell, but immediately made a second attempt. Again it fell, and so on for twelve times, but on the thirteenth attempt succeeded. The King, taking new courage from the example of the spider, rose up and exclaimed: "Have I not been twelve times defeated by the superior force of the enemy? On one fight more hangs the independence of my country." It was only a few days more until he gained the great victory over Edward the third in the battle of Bannockburn.

Read: "The Crow and the Pitcher," from Wiltse's *Kindergarten Stories and Morning Talks.*

Sing: "Try, Try Again," from *Songs Every One Should Know.*

Birthdays: James Cook, an English navigator, born at Marton, Yorkshire, England, October 27, 1728; died February 14, 1779.

Joseph Emerson Worcester, an American author, born in Bedford, N. H., August 24, 1784; died in Cambridge, Mass., October 27, 1865. Chiefly famous for his *A Dictionary of the English Language.*

Whitelaw Reid, an American journalist and diplomatist, born near Xenia, Ohio, October 27, 1837.

Theodore Roosevelt, twenty-sixth president of the United States, born in New York, October 27, 1858; lives in Oyster Bay, Long Island, N. Y.

28 BUILDERS

Little builders, build away!
Little builders, build to-day!
Build a temple pure and bright,
Build it up in deeds of light;
Lay the corner strong and deep,
Where the heart the truth shall keep;
Lay it with a builder's care,
For the temple resteth there.

If you want an honored name,
If you want a spotless fame,
Let your words be kind and pure,
And your temple shall endure;
Wisdom standeth at the door;
·Come and see her priceless store;
Virtue gently guides your feet,
Where the good and holy meet.

—Selected

Read: Bible, Mark 10:43-44.

Sing: "The Fountain," from *Songs Every One Should Know*.

Birthday: Anna Elizabeth Dickinson, an American lecturer and author, born in Philadelphia, Pa., October 28, 1842; lives in New York.

Special Day: Arbor Day in Indiana (last Friday in October). (See *Arbor Day,* April 19 and 20, this book.)

29 HAPPINESS

Laugh, and the world laughs with you;
Weep, and you weep alone;
For this brave old earth must borrow its mirth;
It has trouble enough of its own.

—Ella Wheeler Wilcox

Birthday: John Keats, a noted English poet, born in London, England, October 29, 1795; died at Rome, Italy, February 27, 1821.

30 INDUSTRY

How doth the little busy bee
Improve each shining hour,
And gather honey all the day
From every opening flower?
                    —*Isaac Watts*

THE GRASSHOPPER AND THE BEE

A GRASSHOPPER, cold and hungry, came to a well-stored beehive and humbly begged the bees for a few drops of honey.

One of the bees asked him how he had spent his time all the summer, and why he had not laid up a store of food for the winter.

"Truly," said he, "I spent my time very merrily in drinking, and dancing, and singing, and never thought about the winter."

"Our plan is very different," said the bee. "We work hard in summer, to lay by a store of food against the season when we foresee that we shall need it; but those who do nothing but dance and sing during the summer, must expect to starve in winter."

This fable teaches that if we spend our time in idleness we shall surely come to want. Sloth makes all things difficult, but industry makes all things easy.

Read: "The Ant and the Cricket," from Baldwin's *Fairy Stories and Fables;* "The Beaver Story," from Bakewell's *True Fairy Stories.*

Sing: "The Secret of Success," from *Uncle Sam's School Songs.*

Birthdays: John Adams, second president of the United States, born in Braintree, Mass., October 30, 1735; died at Quincy, Mass., July 4, 1826, his son then being the president.

Adelaide A. Proctor, British poet, born October 30, 1825; died, 1864.

31 HALLOWE'EN

Up the airy mountain,
  Down the rushy glen,
We   daren't   go   a-hunting,
  For fear of little men;
Wee folk, good folk,
  Trooping all together;
Green jacket, red cap,
  And white owl's feather!
  —*Wm. Allingham*

ALL-HALLOW-EVEN [HALLOWE'EN]

The Eve of All Saints' Day

ALL-HALLOW-EVE (or Even) is known in some places as Nutcrack Night, or Snapapple Night. It is now usually celebrated by children's parties, when certain special games are played. In the country towns it is also a time of careless frolic, and of great bonfires.

The custom of keeping the night has come to us from the Celts. The early inhabitants of Great Britain, Ireland, and parts of France were known as Celts, and their religion was directed by strange priests called Druids. Three times in the year, on the first of May, for the sowing; at the solstice, June 21st, for the ripening and turn of the year; and on the eve of November 1st, for the harvesting, those mysterious priests of the Celts, the Druids, built fires on the hill-tops in France, Britain, and Ireland in honor of the sun. This last festival was made a very solemn ceremony, the Druids of all the region gathering in their white robes around the stone altar or cairn on the hill-top. On the sacred cairn—which was a large mound of stones—was a sacred fire, which had been kept burning through the year. The Druids gathered around the fire, and, at a signal, quenched it. Presently a new fire was kindled on the cairn, and as it gleamed in the darkness, the people in the valley raised a great shout and other fires from sur-

rounding hill-tops answered the sacred flame. Then the
people were satisfied, for they believed everything was safe
for another year.

When the Celts were converted to the Christian religion,
the harvest festival of the Druids became in the Catholic
Calendar the Eve of All Saints, for that is the meaning
of the name "All-hallow Eve." The custom of playing
pranks on Hallowe'en came from the old idea that this is
"witches' night," and that all the strange and wild powers
of the air are abroad to do mischief, but just when and
where the thought arose, no one seems to know.

Read: "Tamlane," from Jacobs' *More English Fairy
Tales*.

Sing: "The Brownies," from *Songs in Season*.

Birthday: David Graham Phillips, an American author,
born in Madison, Ind., October 31, 1867; died **January 24,
1911**.

Special Day: Hallowe'en.

NOVEMBER

1 TRUST

The leaves are fading and falling,
  The winds are rough and wild;
The birds have ceased their calling,
  But let me tell you, my child,

Though day by day, as it closes,
  Doth darker and colder grow,
The roots of the bright red roses
  Will keep alive in the snow.
                    —*Alice Cary*

Birthday: Antonio Canova, a famous Italian sculptor, born at Possagno, Italy, November 1, 1757; died in Venice, October 13, 1822.

2 GENEROSITY

The truly generous is the truly wise;
And he who loves not others, lives unblest.
                    —*Horace*

A WAIF'S VIEW OF WEALTH

A LITTLE street waif was once at the house of a great lady, and the childish eyes that had to look so sharply after daily bread were dazzled by signs of splendor on every hand. "Can you get everything you want?" the child asked the mistress of the mansion. "Yes, I think so," was the reply. "Can you buy anything you'd like to have?" The lady answered, "Yes." And the child, who was of a meditative turn of mind, looked at her half pityingly, and said, wonderingly, *"Don't you find it dull?"* To the little keen mind, accustomed to live bird-like from day to day, and to rejoice over a little supply with the delight born of rarity, the aspect of continual plenty, and desires all gratified by possession, contained an idea of monotony that seemed almost wearisome. Many an owner of a well-filled purse has found life "dull," and pronounced in the midst of luxury that all things are vanity; but the hand that knows how wisely to distribute and scatter abroad the bounty possessed will never be without interest in life— will never miss the sunshine that abides for kind and unselfish hearts. —*The Quiver*

Read: "The Elves and the Shoemaker," by Grimm; "Doctor Goldsmith," in Baldwin's *Fifty Famous Stories;* Bible, Psalm 23.

Sing: "Help to Set the World Rejoicing," from *Uncle Sam's School Songs.*

Birthday: James K. Polk, eleventh president of the United States, born in Mecklenberg County, N. C., November 2, 1795; died in Nashville, Tenn., June 15, 1849.

3 THE VALUE OF THINGS

Loveliest of lovely things are they
On earth that soonest pass away.
The rose that lives its little hour
Is prized beyond the sculptured flower.
—*Bryant*

WILLIAM CULLEN BRYANT

To-day is the birthday of William Cullen Bryant, the "poet of nature." He was born in Cummington, Mass. It was soon discovered that the little fellow was very precocious and the parents gave up all hope of his life. But his father being a physician of considerable skill, decided to put William through a severe treatment in order to save his life. So each morning for a long time, summer and winter, the father took his son down to the spring behind the barn and dipped him several times in the cold water. This heroic treatment perhaps saved the child and gave to the world one of its best poets.

Bryant wrote poetry at the age of eight years. In his thirteenth year he wrote a satire on President Jefferson's embargo on American shipping under the title "The Embargo; or Sketches of the Times." In his eighteenth year, his best poem, "Thanatopsis," was written. Bryant was essentially a poet of nature, his verse overflowing with what Wordsworth terms "religion of the woods." After a long and useful life, he died in the "month of roses," according to a wish he had often expressed.

Read: Selections from Bryant's poems.

Sing: "The Song of Nature," from Hanson's *Gems of Song.*

Birthday: William Cullen Bryant, an American poet, born in Cummington, Mass., November 3, 1794; died in New York City, June 12, 1878.

4 PROCRASTINATION

There are no fragments so precious as those of time, and none so heedlessly lost by people who can not make a moment, and yet can waste years.—*Montgomery*

Read: Emerson's "Days;" "What Broke the China Pitcher," from Howliston's *Cat-Tails and Other Tales;* Bible, Eccl. 3:1.

Sing: "Rock of Ages."

Birthdays: James Montgomery, a British poet, born in Ayrshire, Scotland, November 4, 1771; died near Sheffield, Scotland, April 30, 1854.

Augustus M. Toplady, an English clergyman and author, born at Farnham, Surrey, England, November 4, 1740;

died in London, August 11, 1778. Best known as the author
of the hymn, "Rock of Ages."

5 CIVIC DUTY

The proudest now is but my peer,
 The highest not more high;
To-day of all the weary year
 A king of men am I.

To-day alike are great and small,
 The nameless and the known;
My palace is the people's hall,
 The ballot-box my throne!
     —*Whittier*

Special Day: Election or Voting Day (the first Tuesday
after the first Monday in November). This day is now a
holiday, so that every man may have an opportunity to cast
his vote. What are the duties of a voter in a self-governing
country?

1. To vote whenever it is his privilege.
2. To try to understand the questions upon which he votes.
3. To learn something about the character and fitness of the
men for whom he votes.
4. To vote only for honest men for office.
5. To support only honest measures.
6. To give no bribe, direct or indirect, and to receive no bribe
direct or indirect.
7. To place country above party.
8. To recognize the result of the election as the will of the
people and therefore as the law.
9. To continue to vote for a righteous although defeated cause
as long as there is reasonable hope of victory.—*S. E. Forman*

6 LOYALTY TO OUR COUNTRY

Ye who love the Republic, remember the claim
Ye owe to her fortune, ye owe to her fame,
To her years of prosperity, past and in store,
The hundreds behind you, the thousands before.
     —*Hezekiah Butterworth*

THE FLAG GOES BY

BY HENRY H. BENNETT

HATS off!
Along the street there comes
A blare of bugles, a ruffle of drums,
A flash of color beneath the sky.
    Hats off!
The flag is passing by.

Blue and crimson and white it shines
Over the steel-tipped, ordered lines.
    Hats off!
The colors before us fly;
But more than the flag is passing by.

Sea-fights and land-fights, grim and great,
Fought to make and save the state;
Weary marches and sinking ships;
Cheers of victory on dying lips;

Days of plenty and years of peace;
March of a strong land's swift increase;
Equal justice, right and law;
Stately honor and reverent awe,

Sign of a nation, great and strong
To ward her people from foreign wrong,
Pride and glory and honor, all
Live in the colors to stand or fall.

    Hats off!
Along the street there comes
A blare of bugles, a ruffle of drums,
And loyal hearts are beating high.
    Hats off!
The flag is passing by!

Sing: "The Star-Spangled Banner;" play selections from Paderewski.

Birthdays: Kate Greenaway, an English artist noted for her pictures of children and of child life, born in London, England, in 1846; died at London, November 6, 1901.

Ignace Jan Paderewski, a Russian pianist, born in Podolie, Russian Poland, November 6, 1860.

7 AMBITION

> The height of my ambition is only to find my place,
> though it were but a sweeper of chimneys.
> —*Charles Kingsley*

Read: "Don't Give Up" and "Suppose," by Phœbe Cary; "The Two Foolish Birds," from Baldwin's *Fairy Stories and Fables*.

8 NOBLE CONDUCT

> He prayeth well, who loveth well
> Both man and bird and beast.
> He prayeth best who loveth best
> All things both great and small,
> For the dear God who loveth us—
> He made and loveth all.
> —*From "Ancient Mariner" by Coleridge*

HOW BABY ROBIN WAS SAVED

MOTHER ROBIN had built her nest in the eaves of one of the very nicest apartment houses in Chicago. One day Father Robin had some business to attend away from home, so that Mother Robin was forced to go out into the world in search of food and to leave Master Robin alone in his eerie nursery.

And sure enough the baby got into mischief. He wiggled his wings, and zip! down he plunged toward the street. He hit the pavement square in the middle of one of the busiest motoring corners. A chauffeur stopped his big machine abruptly. Other machines behind him halted, and soon a half hundred motor cars were tangled at the corner.

Policemen came and tried to remove the cause of the congestion, but baby robin had just enough strength left in his wings to dodge. A policeman then called a small boy to his aid. That settled Master Robin's holiday. The boy nabbed him in a twinkling, and soon the little robin was back in his nest.

9 THOROUGHNESS

Work while you work, play while you play;
This is the way to be cheerful and gay.
All that you do, do with your might;
Things done by halves are never done right.

One thing each time, and that done well,
Is a very good rule, as many can tell;
Moments are useless, trifled away;
So work while you work, and play while you play.
—*Miss A. D. Stoddart*

10 TRUE WORTH

Four things a man must learn to do,
If he would make his calling true,—
To think without confusion clearly,
To love his fellow-men sincerely,
To act from honest motives purely,
To trust in God and heaven securely.
—*Henry Van Dyke*

TWO MEN OF WORTH

IN SWITZERLAND, many years ago, a man called Frank went to his neighbor, William, who was working in his field, and said: "Friend, I have received word that we are to go before the judges to-morrow, who will decide our dispute about the field, since we cannot agree ourselves."

"You see," said William, "that I have mown this field and must get my hay in; I cannot leave it."

"Well," said Frank, "I cannot send the judges away."

They discussed the matter for some time. At length

William said: "I will tell you how it shall be: you go to the judges and tell them your case and mine; then there will be no need for me to go."

"Well," said the other, "if you will trust your cause with me, I will do so."

He accordingly went, pleaded the case, and lost. Returning to his neighbor, he said: "The field is yours. I congratulate you, neighbor. I am glad the affair is over."

The two men were firm friends ever after.

Read: "The Farmer and His Sons," and "The Quarrel," from Baldwin's *Fairy Stories and Fables*.

Sing: "Morning Song," from Kellogg's *Best Primary Songs*.

Birthdays: Martin Luther, the leader of the Reformation in Germany, born at Eisleben, Germany, November 10, 1483; died at Eisleben, February 18, 1546.

Oliver Goldsmith, a famous English author, born in Pallasmore, Ireland, November 10, 1728; died in London, England, April 4, 1774.

Johann Christoph Friedrich von Schiller, a famous German poet, born at Marbach, Würtemberg, November 10, 1759; died at Weimar, May 9, 1805.

Joaquin Miller, the pen-name of Cincinnatus Heine Miller, an American author, born in Wabash District, Indiana, November 10, 1841.

Henry Van Dyke, an American clergyman and author, born at Germantown, Pa., November 10, 1852; lives in Princeton, N. J.

Winston Churchill, an American novelist, born in St. Louis, Mo., November 10, 1871; living at Cornish, N. H.

11 HUMILITY

For praise too dearly loved, or warmly sought,
Enfeebles all internal strength of thought;
And the weak soul within itself unblest,
Leans for all pleasure on another's breast.
—*Goldsmith*

STOOP AS YOU GO THROUGH

Benjamin Franklin, the son of a tallow-chandler, the printer's apprentice, the printer, the philosopher, and the patriot, wrote the following incident of his visit, when a young man, to the celebrated Cotton Mather, a clergyman of New England. The letter was written to Cotton Mather's son.

"The last time I saw your father was in the beginning of 1724, when I visited him after my first trip to Pennsylvania. He received me in the library, and, on my taking leave, showed me a shorter way out of his house, through a narrow passage, which was crossed by a beam overhead. We were still talking as I withdrew, he accompanying behind, and I turning partly toward him, when he said hastily, 'Stoop, stoop!' I did not understand him till I felt my head hit against the beam. He was a man that never missed any occasion of giving instruction; and, upon this, he said, 'You are young, and have the world before you. Stoop as you go through it, and you will miss many hard thumps.' This advice, thus beat into my head, has frequently been of use to me; and I often think of it when I see pride mortified, and misfortunes brought upon people by carrying their heads too high." Before honor is humility.

Birthday: Thomas Bailey Aldrich, an American poet and novelist, born in Portsmouth, N. H., November 11, 1836; died in Boston, Mass., March 19, 1907.

12 FORGIVENESS

He that cannot forgive others, breaks the bridge over which he must pass himself; for every man has need to be forgiven.—*Lord Herbert*

A QUARREL SOON ENDED

Two dogs began to quarrel over a bone that had been thrown to one of them. They were fighting on a bridge

and before they knew it, both had fallen into the water.
One of them was a Newfoundland dog, and swam easily
to shore, but when he looked for his enemy he saw him still
struggling in the water. This dog could not swim, and he
was about to drown, when the Newfoundland dog plunged
in and brought him safely to shore. They forgave each
other then and became great friends.

Read: ''The Sympathy of Abraham Lincoln'' and ''A
Hero of Valley Forge,'' from Baldwin's *An American
Book of Golden Deeds;* Bible, Matt. 5: 7-9 and 43-48.
Sing: ''Good Advice,'' from *Merry Melodies.*

13 HAPPINESS

Happy hearts and happy faces,
Happy play in grassy places—
That was how, in ancient ages,
Children grew to kings and sages.
—*Robert Louis Stevenson*

PRAYER AT MORNING

BY ROBERT LOUIS STEVENSON

THE day returns and brings us the petty round of irritat-
ing concerns and duties. Help us to perform them with
laughter and kind faces, let cheerfulness abound with
industry. Give us to go blithely on our business all this
day, bring us to our resting beds weary and content and
undishonored, and grant us in the end the gift of sleep.

Read: Selections from Stevenson's *A Child's Garden of
Verses.*
Sing: Selections from *Robert Louis Stevenson Songs.*
Birthdays: Joseph Hooker, an American general, born
in Hadley, Mass., November 13, 1814; died at Garden City,
N. Y., October 31, 1879.
Edwin Thomas Booth, a noted American tragic actor,

born at Bel Air, Md., November 13, 1833; died June 7, 1893. (John Wilkes Booth (1839-1865), a younger brother, was the assassin of President Lincoln.)

Robert Louis Stevenson, a noted Scottish novelist and story writer, born in Edinburgh, Scotland, November 13, 1850; died at Apia, Samoa, December 3, 1894.

14   SELF-CONTROL

How happy is he born or taught,
Whose passions not his master are;
Lord of himself, though not of lands,
And having nothing, yet hath all!
—*Sir Henry Wotton*

THE ECHO

LITTLE PETER had never heard of the Echo which lives among the woods and rocks, and repeats the very words we speak. One day while walking in a field near a wood, he saw a squirrel running among the bushes. "Ho! Stop there!" he cried. Something in the woods answered him back, "Ho! Stop there!" Astonished, Peter shouted out, "Who are you?" The word came back, "Who are you?"— "You are a fool," he answered. "You are a fool," was echoed back loud and clear from the wood. Peter grew angry, for he thought some saucy boy was hidden behind the trees. Then he poured out all the hard ugly names he could think of, but the Echo sent them all back to him in mocking tones.

"He shall learn not to call me names," he said to himself, as he picked up a stick and ran toward the wood. Peter wandered in the wood a long time, but found no one. Tired and vexed, he went home and complained to his mother that a naughty boy, who had been calling him names, was hiding in the wood.

"You have been angry with your own self," said his

mother. "It was only your own voice that made the sound, and you heard only the echo of your own words. If you had spoken kind words, kind words would have come back to you from the wood."

—*White's School Management*

15 SERVICE

Not what we give, but what we share,
For the gift without the giver is bare;
Who gives himself with his alms feeds three,—
Himself, his hungering neighbor, and me.
—*Lowell*

Birthdays: William Pitt, first earl of Chatham, an English statesman, born November 15, 1708; died at Hayes, Kent, England, May 11, 1778.

Sir William Herschel, a noted English astronomer, born in Hanover, Prussia, November 15, 1738; died at his home at Slough, near Windsor, England, August 23, 1822.

16 TRUTH

Dare to be true; nothing can need a lie.
A fault which needs it most grows two thereby.
—*George Herbert*

THE PRICE OF A LIE

IF WE are under no moral obligation to fulfill a promise made to do a wrong, there can be no dishonor in refusing its performance. Dishonor belongs to those who persist in doing wrong after they have discovered the right.

"Would you tell a lie for three cents?" asked a teacher of one of her boys. "No, ma'am," answered Dick, very promptly. "For ten cents?" "No, ma'am." "For a dollar?" "No, ma'am." "For a hundred dollars?" "No, ma'am." "For a thousand dollars?"

Here Dick was staggered. A thousand dollars looked like such a very big sum. Oh! what lots of things he could buy with a thousand dollars. While he was thinking about it, and trying to make up his mind whether it would pay to tell a lie for a thousand dollars, a boy behind him cried out: "No, ma'am." "Why not?" asked the teacher.

Now, mark this boy's answer, and do not forget it. "Because, ma'am," said he, "*the lie sticks*. When the thousand dollars are all gone, and the good things bought with them are all gone, too, the lie is there all the same."

And when we tell a lie we never can tell where the injury that springs from it will stop. It is just like loosening a great rock at the top of a mountain and letting it go rolling and plunging down the side of the mountain. Nobody can tell how far it will go, nor how much injury it will do before it stops rolling.

Read: "Little Scotch Granite," from White's *School Management*.

17 HUMILITY

The very flowers that bend and meet,
In sweetening others grow more ,sweet.
—Holmes

18 JUSTICE

Be just and fear not;
Let all the ends thou aim'st at be thy country's,
Thy God's, and truth's.
—Shakespeare

Read: "The Bell of Atri," from Baldwin's *Fifty Famous Stories Retold*.

Birthdays: Asa Gray, an American botanist, born in Paris, Oneida County, N. Y., November 18, 1810; died at Cambridge, Mass., January 30, 1888.

William S. Gilbert, an English dramatist, born in London, England, November 18, 1836; drowned at Harrow, England, May 29, 1911.

19 WISDOM

Next 'in importance to freedom and justice is popular education, without which neither justice nor freedom can be permanently maintained.—*James A. Garfield*

THE CAREFUL OBSERVER

BY COLTON

A DERVISH was journeying alone in a desert, when two merchants suddenly met him. "You have lost a camel," said he to the merchants. "Indeed we have," they replied.

"Was he not blind in his right eye, and lame in his left leg?" said the dervish. "He was," replied the merchants. "Had he not lost a front tooth?" "He had," said the merchants. "And was he not loaded with honey on one side, and with corn on the other?" "Most certainly he was," they replied; "and, as you have seen him so lately, and marked him so particularly, you can, in all probability, conduct us to him."

"My friends," said the dervish, "I have never seen your camel, nor ever heard of him, but from you!" "A pretty story, truly," said the merchants; "but where are the jewels which formed a part of his burden?" "I have seen neither your camel nor your jewels," repeated the dervish.

On this, they seized his person, and forthwith hurried him before the cadi; but, on the strictest search, nothing could be found upon him, nor could any evidence whatever be adduced to convict him either of falsehood or of theft.

They were about to proceed against him as a sorcerer, when the dervish, with great calmness, thus addressed the court: "I have been much amused with your surprise, and own that there has been some ground for your suspicions; but I have lived long and alone, and I can find ample scope for observation even in a desert.

"I knew that I had crossed the track of a camel that had strayed from its owner, because I saw no mark of any human footstep on the same route. I knew that the animal was blind of one eye, because it had cropped the herbage only on one side of its path; and that it was lame in one leg, from the faint impression which that particular foot had produced upon the sand.

"I concluded that the animal had lost one tooth, because, wherever it had grazed, a small tuft of herbage had been left uninjured in the center of its bite. As to that which formed the burden of the beast, the busy ants informed me that it was corn on the one side; and the clustering flies, that it was honey on the other."

Birthdays: Albert Bertel Thorwaldsen, a Danish sculptor, born at sea, November 19, 1770; died in Copenhagen, Denmark, March 24, 1844.

James A. Garfield, an American general and statesman, and twentieth president of the United States, born in Orange, Ohio, November 19, 1831; shot by an assassin in Washington, D. C., July 2, 1881.

20 MOTHER

Hundreds of stars in the silent sky,
Hundreds of shells on the shore together,
Hundreds of birds that go singing by,
Hundreds of bees in the sunny weather;
Hundreds of dewdrops to greet the dawn,
Hundreds of lambs in the purple clover,
Hundreds of butterflies on the lawn—
But only *one mother* the wide world over.

Birthday: Peregrine White, the first child of English parents born in New England, born on the Mayflower, November 20, 1620; he died July 20, 1704.

21 PATRIOTISM

He who serves his country well has no need of ancestors.—*Voltaire*

Read: "William Tell," from Baldwin's *Fifty Famous Stories Retold;* "Lexington," by Holmes.

Sing: "America."

Birthday: Francois Marie Arouet de Voltaire, a famous French writer, born in Paris, France, November 21, 1694; died in Paris, May 30, 1778.

22   PATIENCE

It is easy finding reasons why other folks should be patient.—*George Eliot*

PEGGING AWAY DID IT

A FRIEND once said to President Lincoln: "Do you expect to end this war during your administration?" Mr. Lincoln replied: "I do not know, sir." "But Mr. Lincoln, what do you mean to do?" "Peg away, sir; peg away, keep pegging away!" Pegging away did it.

Read: "Wait and See," from Poulsson's *In the Child's World.* "The Little Rooster," from *Boston Collection of Kindergarten Stories.*

Birthday: Robert Cavelier de La Salle, a noted French navigator, born in Rouen, France, November 22, 1643; shot when near a branch of the Trinity River in Texas, March 19, 1687.

Philip Schuyler, an American general, born at Albany, N. Y., November 22, 1733; died at Albany, November 18, 1804.

George Eliot, the assumed name of Mary Ann Evans, a famous English writer of novels, born at Arbury Farm, Derbyshire, England, November 22, 1819; died December 22, 1880.

23   HONOR

Honor and shame from no condition rise,
Act well your part, there all the honor lies.
—Pope

Birthday: Franklin Pierce, the fourteenth president of the United States, born in Hillsborough, N. H., November 23, 1804; died in Concord, Mass., October 8, 1869.

Special Days: Arbor Day in South Carolina (third Friday in November).

Arbor Day in West Virginia (third Friday in November and April). (See *Arbor Day*, April 19 and 20, this book.)

24 HEROISM

Heroism is simple, and yet it is rare. Every one who does the best he can is a hero.—*Josh Billings*

GRACE DARLING

To-day is the birthday of Grace Darling, an English girl, who did so brave a deed that her name is known wherever the English language is spoken. The desolate Farne Islands lie off the northeast coast of Northumberland—a group of stern basaltic rocks, black and bare, with a dangerous sea roaring about them. In stormy weather they are inaccessible for days and weeks together. They have no other inhabitants but the gulls and puffins that scream about the rocks. But on the farthest point, the Longstone Rock, a lighthouse had been erected to warn off the ships passing between England and Scotland. Two old persons— a man and his wife—and a young woman, their daughter— Grace Darling—were the keepers of the lighthouse.

One night in September, 1838, a steamer was wrecked near the lighthouse, and in the morning Grace saw some people clinging to the rocks or to the fragments of the vessel. The fog was so heavy and the sea so rough that Mr. Darling was afraid to go to the rescue, but Grace persuaded him to launch a boat. Then followed the greatest struggle of their lives. The wind beat against them, the waves dashed over them, but they cared not for all this.

When they reached the wrecked vessel, only nine of the sixty-three unfortunate beings were alive. These they took into their boat and started on the return trip. The rescued men were so weak with cold and hunger and thirst that not one was able to use an oar, and it was only after a terrible struggle that Grace and her father were able to reach their lighthouse home. There the mother was ready to receive them, to nurse them, to feed them, and to restore them to health and strength. They remained there for three days, until the storm abated, and they could be carried to the mainland. For this brave act a subscription of £700 ($3,500) was raised for Grace Darling, and she received many other valuable presents. When she died her friends placed a marble monument over her grave.

Read: Wordsworth's "Grace Darling."

Birthdays: Zachary Taylor, general and twelfth president of the United States, born in Orange County, Va., November 24, 1784; died in Washington, D. C., July 9, 1850.

Grace Darling, an English heroine, born at Bamborough, Northumberland, November 24, 1815; died October 20, 1842.

Frances Hodgson Burnett, an American novelist, born in Manchester, England, November 24, 1849; living in Washington, D. C. Best known to young folks by her beautiful story called *Little Lord Fauntleroy*.

25 HONESTY

He that cannot think is a fool;
He that will not think is a bigot;
He that dare not is a slave.
—*Carnegie*

THE STORY OF ANDREW CARNEGIE

THERE was once a young Scotch boy, the son of a weaver. He was born poor, in a story-and-a-half house. He came to this country with the rest of his father's family when he was ten, and commenced on a job that paid him 20 cents a day.

Faithful work as a bobbin boy soon procured him a position that earned him almost a dollar a day. His attentiveness to what was given him to do brought him after a little while to the attention of a railroad man who was a large employer of help.

He had in the meantime been economizing his small earnings, out of which it was suggested to him that he take a little stock in a car company. He hadn't enough money and no security to offer, but resolved to apply to the bank for a loan.

What happened when he went to the bank is what I want the boys particularly to notice, for it really marks the crisis in the young fellow's life and explains what followed during the years after.

I just said that in asking for a loan he had nothing that he could offer as security; that is, he owned nothing that he could make over to the bank in case he failed to return the loan. Security of the ordinary kind he did not have, but he had something that was just as satisfactory to the banker, for he had a character for honesty, faithfulness and perseverance, and the banker said to him: "You shall have the money, Andy."

That $600 was the turning point in Andrew Carnegie's life and was the nest-egg that in course of time filled the nest with so many eggs that it would take a string of figures to count them.—*Adapted from Dr. Charles H. Parkhurst*

Sing: "You Never Miss the Water," from Uncle Sam's School Songs.

Birthdays: John Bigelow, an American editor and diplomatist, born in Malden, Ulster County, N. Y., November 25, 1817; died December 19, 1911.

Andrew Carnegie, an American capitalist and philanthropist, born in Dunfermline, Scotland, November 25, 1835.

26   THANKSGIVING

And we, to-day, amidst our flowers
  And fruits, have come to own again
The blessings of the summer hours,
  The early and the latter rain;
To see our Father's hand once more
  Reverse for us the plenteous horn
Of autumn, filled and running o'er
  With fruit, and flower, and golden corn!
                              —*Whittier*

Read: "The Landing of the Pilgrims," by Felicia
Hemans; "The First Thanksgiving Day," from Wiggin
and Smith's *The Story Hour;* "How Patty Gave Thanks,"
from Poulsson's *In the Child's World;* "The Story of the
First Corn," from Bailey and Lewis' *For the Children's
Hour;* Bible, Psalm 100. For Thanksgiving selections, procure a copy of Sindelar's *Thanksgiving Entertainments.*

Sing: "Thanksgiving Day" and "Thanksgiving Joys,"
from *Songs in Season.*

Birthday: William Cowper, a noted English poet, born
in Hertfordshire, England, November 26, 1731; died at
East Dereham, Norfolk, England, April 25, 1800.

Special Day: Thanksgiving Day (last Thursday in
November).

27   THANKSGIVING

[Continued]

Over the river and through the wood
To grandfather's house we'll go:
The horse knows the way
To carry the sleigh
Through the white and drifted snow.

Over the river and through the wood,
Trot fast, my dapple gray!
Spring over the ground
Like a hunting hound!
For this is Thanksgiving Day.
                              —*Selected*

28 FRIENDSHIP

When you find one good and true,
Change not the old friend for the new.

Birthday: Anton Rubinstein, a famous Russian pianist and composer, born in Volhynia, Russia, November 28, 1829; died at Peterhof, Russia, November 20, 1894.

29 FAITHFULNESS

Faithfulness in little things fits one for heroism when the great trials come.—*Louisa May Alcott*

Read: Selections from the *Louisa Alcott Reader*.

Birthdays: Wendell Phillips, a noted American orator, born in Boston, Mass., November 29, 1811; died in Boston, February 2, 1884.

Louisa May Alcott, an American author, born in Germantown, Pa., November 29, 1832; died in Concord, Mass., March 6, 1888.

30 PERSEVERANCE

My son, observe the postage stamp! Its usefulness depends upon its ability to stick to one thing until it gets there.—*Josh Billings*

THE LAYING OF THE TELEGRAPH-CABLE

CYRUS W. FIELD became a clerk in New York when fifteen years old, and in a few years was at the head of a large mercantile house. When he got rich he gave up his business, and devoted himself to a plan for the laying of a telegraphic cable under the ocean between Europe and America. The first two attempts were disappointments; the third time was successful, and several messages were flashed across. Everybody rejoiced, but in a little while the messages stopped, the cable ceased working, and people began to say that it never could be laid. Field alone kept up a brave heart. Seven years passed by, and the *Great Eastern* steamed off with a new cable; but soon the ill tidings came that by a sudden lurch of the ship the cable was broken in mid-ocean. After this people lost all patience with Field's plans, but with the resolved will of a hero, he succeeded in 1866 in uniting the two hemispheres, amid the rejoicings and congratulations of the world. He accomplished his purpose because he would not give up. When the cable was laid, Mr. Field said of his trials: "It has been a long and hard struggle to lay the Atlantic telegraph —nearly thirteen years of anxious watching and ceaseless toil. Often has my heart been ready to sink. I have sometimes almost accused myself of madness for sacrificing all my home comforts for what might, after all, prove a dream. I have seen my companions one after another fall by my side, and feared that I, too, might not live to see the end. I have often prayed that I might not taste of death till this work was accomplished. That prayer is now answered."

Sing: "Work, for the Night is Coming" or "Life is Real, Life is Earnest," from *Uncle Sam's School Songs*.

Birthdays: Jonathan Swift, a British writer, born in Dublin, Ireland, November 30, 1667, of English ancestry; died October 19, 1735. Author of *Gulliver's Travels*.

Cyrus W. Field, an American merchant, famous for laying the telegraph-cable between Europe and America, born in Stockbridge, Mass., November 30, 1819; died July 11, 1892.

Mark Twain, the pen-name of Samuel Langhorne Clemens, a noted American author and humorist, born at Florida, Mo., November 30, 1835; died at his summer home in Reading Ridge, Conn., April 21, 1910.

DECEMBER

1 FLATTERY

Flattery is like a painted armor; only for show.
—*Socrates*

FLATTERERS AND SLANDERERS

THE response of Diogenes, the ancient Greek philosopher, to the question, "What beast's bite is the most dangerous?" was "If you mean wild beasts, the slanderer's; if tame ones, the flatterer's."

Birthday: Clarke Mills, an American sculptor, born in Onondaga County, N. Y., December 1, 1815; died in Washington, D. C., January 12, 1883.

Special Day: Arbor Day in Georgia (first Friday in December). (See *Arbor Day*, April 19 and 20, this book.)

2 PURPOSE

But whatever you are, be true, boys!
Be visible through and through, boys!
Leave to others the shamming,
The cheating and palming,
In fun and in earnest, be true, boys!
—*Mackay*

"WHAT SHALL I DO?"

"WHAT shall I do?" My boy, don't stand asking;
Take hold of something—whatever you can;
Don't turn aside for the toiling or tasking;
Idle, soft hands never yet made a man.

Grasp with a will whatever needs doing;
　Still stand ready, when one work is done,
Another to seize, then still pursuing
　In duty your course, find the victory won.

Do your best for to-day, trust God for to-morrow;
　Don't be afraid of a jest or a sneer;
Be cheerful and hopeful, and no trouble borrow;
　Keep the heart true, and the head cool and clear.

If you can climb to the top without falling,
　Do it. If not, go as high as you can.
Man is not honored by business or calling;
　Business and calling are honored by man.

　　　　　　　　　　　　　　　　　—Selected

Sing: "Good Resolutions," from *Uncle Sam's School Songs.*

Birthdays: Hernando Cortes, the conqueror of Mexico, born in Medellin, Spain, in 1485; died near Seville, Spain, December 2, 1547.

Richard Montgomery, an American general, born near Raphoe, Ireland, December 2, 1736; killed by a cannon-ball, December 31, 1775.

3   TRUE WORTH

True worth is in *being*, not *seeming*,—
　In doing each day that goes by
Some little good—not in the dreaming
　Of great things to do by and by.
For whatever men say in blindness,
　And spite of the fancies of youth,
There's nothing so kingly as kindness,
　And nothing so royal as truth.

　　　　　　　　　　　　　　　—Alice Cary

ROBERT BURNS AND THE FARMER

ROBERT BURNS was once taken to task by a young Edinburgh nobleman, with whom he was walking, for recognizing an honest farmer in the street. "Why, you fantastic gomeral!" exclaimed Burns, "it was not the great coat, the scone bonnet, and the saunders-boot hose that I spoke to, but *the man* that was in them; and the man, sir, for true worth, would weigh down you and me, and ten more such, any day."

Read: "The Magnet's Choice," from Howliston's *Cat-Tails and Other Tales;* "Naughty Little Gold Finger," from *Boston Collection of Kindergarten Stories,* Bible, Prov. 22: 1-2.

Sing: "The Fountain," from *Songs Every One Should Know.*

Birthdays: Mary Baker Glover Eddy, the founder of Christian Science, born at Bow, N. H., July 16, 1821; died December 3, 1910.

George B. McClellan, an American general, born in Philadelphia, Pa., December 3, 1826; died at Orange, N. J., October 29, 1885.

4 WORK

There is always hope in a man that actually and earnestly works. In idleness alone is there perpetual despair.—*Carlyle*

Birthday: Thomas Carlyle, an English author, born in Ecclefechan, Scotland, December 4, 1795; died in Chelsea, London, England, February 5, 1881.

5 YOUTH

My boy, I'd give the world, if it were mine,
To backward turn the dial of time
And be a boy again, with heart like thine;
To quaff again the cup, care free—
To play the pranks that thou dost play on me,
And laugh the laugh the boyhood's sportive glee;
To chase each gold-winged butterfly I meet,
To feel the green grass kiss my sun-browned feet,
To look on life as but a poem sweet.

Be not too swift to run thy boyish race—
Too soon will come the time, though slow the pace,
When care will mark its furrows on thy face.
Youth comes but once; we may not change the plan;
Enjoy these days—the only ones that can
Reward the sufferings of the grown-up man.
—*A. E. Jackson*

Sing: "Follow Me, Full of Glee," from Kellogg's *Best Primary Songs.*

Birthday: Martin Van Buren, eighth president of the United States, born at Kinderhook, N. Y., December 5, 1782; died at Kinderhook, July 24, 1862.

George A. Custer, an American soldier, born at New Rumley, Ohio, December 5, 1839; killed while in command of an expedition against the Sioux Indians, June 25, 1876.

6 USEFULNESS

No one is useless in this world who lightens the burden of another.—*Dickens*

LITTLE THINGS

BY EBENEZER C. BREWER

LITTLE drops of water,
    Little grains of sand,
Make the mighty ocean,
    And the pleasant land.

Thus the little minutes
    Humble though they be,
Make the mighty ages
    Of eternity.

7 UNKIND WORDS

Oh, many a shaft at random sent
Finds mark the archer little meant,
And many a word at random spoken
May soothe, or wound a heart that's broken.
—*Scott*

A DINNER OF TONGUES

ÆSOP was the servant of a philosopher named Xanthus. One day his master being desirous of entertaining some of his friends to dinner, he ordered him to provide the best things he could find in the market. Æsop thereupon made a large provision of *tongues,* which he had the cook serve up with different sauces. When dinner came, all the courses and side dishes were of tongues.

"Did I not order you," said Xanthus, in a violent passion, "to buy the *best* victuals which the market afforded?"

"And have I not obeyed your orders?" said Æsop. "Is there anything better than tongues? Is not the tongue the bond of civil society, the key of science, and the organ of truth and reason? It is by means of the tongue cities are built, and governments established and administered; with it men instruct, persuade, and preside in assemblies."

"Well, then," replied Xanthus, "go to market to-morrow and buy me the *worst* things you can find. This same company shall dine with me, and I have a mind to change my entertainment."

When Xanthus assembled his friends the next day, he was astonished to find that Æsop had provided nothing but the very same dishes.

"Did I not tell you," said Xanthus, "to purchase the *worst* things for this day's feast? How comes it, then, that you have placed before us the same kind of food, which only yesterday, you declared to be the very best?"

Æsop, not at all abashed, replied: "The tongue is the *worst* thing in the world as well as the *best;* for it is the instrument of all strife and contention, the fomenter of law-suits, the source of division and war, the organ of error, of calumny, of falsehood, and even of profanity."

Read: "The Fairy Who Judged Her Neighbors," from Ingelow's *Three Fairy Stories.*

8 PERSEVERANCE

If little labor, little are our gains;
Man's fortunes are according to his pains.
—*Herrick*

ELI WHITNEY AND THE COTTON-GIN

ELI WHITNEY when a boy earned his living by making nails by hand. By careful economy he was enabled to pay his way through Yale College, from which he graduated in 1792. He then went to Georgia to become a tutor, but found the expected place filled, and accordingly sought employment on the plantation of the widow of General Nathaniel Greene, near Savannah. There he developed much' inventive talent, and at Mrs. Greene's suggestion undertook to devise a machine which would do the work of cleaning cotton and separating it from the seed. He devoted a winter to the task, and the result was the machine which he called the cotton-gin. This machine would do in a few days the work which it formerly took a hundred men many weeks to do. When the machine was perfected, in 1793, he showed it to nobody but Mrs. Greene and one other person, but it soon became talked about, the building which contained it was broken open at night and the model was stolen. Before he could make another and get a patent upon it, several of the machines were at work on neighboring plantations. This theft compelled him to resort to many law-suits in a vain effort to protect his rights. The net result was that Mr. Whitney never received any fair return for one of the greatest inventions of the age and one which did more for the Southern States than any other. Thus robbed by his beneficiaries, Mr. Whitney returned to New England in 1798, and engaged in the manufacture of firearms, in which he was very successful.

Birthdays: Eli Whitney, inventor of the cotton-gin, born in Westborough, Mass., December 8, 1765; died in New Haven, Conn., January 8, 1825.

George Alfred Henty, an English writer of novels and stories for young folks, born at Trumpington, near Cambridge, England, December 8, 1832; died November 16, 1902.

Björnstjerne Björnson, a famous Norwegian dramatist and novelist, born at Koikne, Osterdalen, Norway, December 8, 1832; died in Paris, France, April 26, 1910.

Joel Chandler Harris, an American writer, born at Eatonton, Ga., December 8, 1848; died in Atlanta, Ga., July 3, 1908.

9 COURAGE

Mortals, that would follow me,
Love Virtue; she alone is free;
She can teach you how to climb,
Higher than the sphery chime;
Or, if Virtue feeble were,
Heaven itself would stoop to her.
—*From "Comus" by John Milton*

JOHN MILTON, THE BLIND POET

THE life of John Milton stands as a monument of courage and inspiration, and teaches us a valuable lesson. For six years blindness had been coming upon Milton, and the year of 1660 saw him deprived of sight, and with no support for himself or family. Then he wrote his greatest work, the sublime poem of "Paradise Lost." His "Paradise Regained" was written four years later.

Read: Extracts from Helen Keller's *Story of My Life,* or tell the story to the children; also read her book, *The World I Live In.*

Sing: "Merrily, Merrily Sing," from Kellogg's *Best Primary Songs.*

Birthday: John Milton, a famous English poet, born in London, England, December 9, 1608; died Nov. 8, 1674.

10 HOME AND PARENTS

The boys that are wanted are loving boys,
  Fond of home and father and mother,
Counting the old-fashioned household joys
  Dearer and sweeter than any other.

The girls that are wanted are home girls,
  Girls that are mother's right hand,
That fathers and brothers can trust too,
  And the little ones understand.

Birthday: Edward Eggleston, an American author, born
at Vevay, Ind., December 10, 1837; died at Joshua's Rock,
Lake George, N. Y., September 2, 1902. Author of *The
Hoosier Schoolmaster, The Hoosier Schoolboy*, etc.

Special Day: Arbor Day in Mississippi. (See *Arbor
Day,* April 21 and 22, this book.)

11 GOOD DEEDS

You cannot dream yourself into a character, you
must forge one.—*Carter*

WHICH LOVED BEST

BY JOY ALLISON

"I LOVE you, mother," said little John;
Then forgetting his work, his cap went on,
And he was off to the garden swing,
Leaving his mother the wood to bring.

"I love you, mother," said little Nell,
"I love you better than tongue can tell."
Then she teased and pouted half the day,
Till mother rejoiced when she went to play.

"I love you, mother," said little Fan,
"To-day I'll help you all I can."
To the cradle then she did softly creep,
And rocked the baby till it fell asleep.

Then stepping softly she took the broom
And swept the floor and dusted the room.
Busy and happy all day was she,
Helpful and cheerful as child could be.

"I love you, mother," again they said,
Three little children going to bed.
How do you think the mother guessed
Which of them really loved her best?

Birthday: Sir David Brewster, a famous British philosopher and scholar, born at Jedburgh, Scotland December 11, 1781; died February 10, 1868.

12 AMIABILITY

It's easy enough to be pleasant,
When life flows along like a song;
But the man worth while
Is the one who can smile
When everything goes dead wrong.
—*Ella Wheeler Wilcox*

Birthdays: John Jay, the first chief justice of the United States, born in New York City, December 12, 1745; died at Bedford, N. Y., May 17, 1829.

John R. Green, a noted English historian, born at Oxford, England, December 12, 1837; died at Mentone, France, March 7, 1883.

13 SUCCESS

Set yourself earnestly to see what you were made to do, and then set yourself earnestly to do it.
—*Phillips Brooks*

THE ONE ROAD

"THERE is but one straight road to success," says Bourke Cochran, the well-known orator, "and that is merit. Capacity never lacks opportunity. It cannot remain undiscovered because it is sought by too many anxious to utilize it. A capable man on earth is more valuable than any precious deposit under the earth, and is the object of a more vigilant search.''

Birthdays: Phillips Brooks, a bishop of the Episcopal Church and a noted pulpit orator and poet, born in Boston, Mass., December 13, 1835; died in Boston, January 23, 1893.

Samuel Smiles, a Scottish writer, born at Haddington, Scotland, December 13, 1812; died in England, April 17, 1904.

14   CHEERFULNESS

Be still, sad heart! and cease repining;
Behind the clouds is the sun still shining;
Thy fate is the common fate of all,
Into each life some rain must fall,
    Some days must be dark and dreary.
—*From "The Rainy Day" by Longfellow*

Read: ''The Desert,'' from Richards' *The Golden Windows;* ''The Miller of the Dee,'' from Baldwin's *Fifty Famous Stories Retold.*

Sing: ''Music Everywhere,'' from *Merry Melodies.*

Birthday: Noah Porter, an American writer and scholar, president of Yale College, born in Farmington, Conn., December 14, 1811; died March 4, 1892. Dr. Porter was chief editor of *Webster's International Dictionary.*

15   SERVICE

Men and things are only valuable as they are ' serviceable.

SOMEBODY

Somebody did a golden deed;
Somebody proved a friend in need;
Somebody sang a beautiful song;
Somebody smiled the whole day long;

Somebody thought, " 'Tis sweet to live";
Somebody said, "I'm glad to give";
Somebody fought a valiant fight;
Somebody lived to shield the right;
Was that "Somebody" you?

Read: "Home" and "The Wheatfield," from Richards' *The Golden Windows;* Bible, Matt. 7:12 and Matt. 5:7.

Sing: "The World is What We Make It," from *School Song Knapsack.*

Birthday: Alexandre Gustave Eiffel, a noted French engineer and builder of the Eiffel Tower for the Paris exhibition of 1889, born at Dijon, France, December 15, 1832.

Special Day: Arbor Day in Arkansas. (See *Arbor Day,* April 19 and 20, this book.)

16 TRUE NOBILITY

We want no kings but kings of toil—
No crowns but crowns of deeds;
Not royal birth but sterling worth
Must mark the man who leads.
—*Ella Wheeler Wilcox*

PROOFS OF NOBILITY

BEETHOVEN [birthday December 17], the great musician and composer, who, in his majestic stateliness, is likened to the poet Milton, was asked to produce proofs of his nobility. Turning at once to the king, for the incident occurred at court, the democratic nobleman replied by pointing to his head and his heart, saying, "My nobility is here and here."

17 WHITTIER'S BIRTHDAY

The riches of the Commonwealth
Are free, strong minds, and hearts of health;
And more to her than gold or grain,
The cunning hand and cultured brain.
—*Whittier*

Read or tell: The story of Whittier's boyhood, life, and work; read the chapters on Quaker life in *Uncle Tom's Cabin;* "Whittier," from Cody's *Four American Poets;* "The Boyhood of John Greenleaf Whittier," from *Our Holidays: Retold from St. Nicholas.* From his poems: "The Barefoot Boy," "Snow-Bound," etc.

Read: "Sir Humphry Davy's Greatest Discovery, Michael Faraday," from Marden's *Stories from Life.*

Sing: "Whittier," from *Songs in Season.*

Birthdays: Ludwig van Beethoven, a famous musician, born in Bonn, Germany, December 17, 1770; died in Vienna, Austria, March 26, 1827.

Sir Humphry Davy, a celebrated English chemist, born in Penzance, Cornwall, England, December 17, 1778; died in Geneva, Switzerland, May 29, 1829.

John Greenleaf Whittier, the "Quaker poet," born in Haverhill, Mass., December 17, 1807; died at Hampton Falls, N. H., September 7, 1892.

18 CONTENTMENT

Over my shaded doorway,
  Two little brown-winged birds
Have chosen to fashion their dwelling
  And utter their loving words.
All day they are coming and going
  On errands frequent and fleet,
And warbling over and over,
  Sweet, sweet, sweet, O, sweet!
                    —*Selected*

THE KING STORK

THERE were once some frogs which lived in a beautiful lake. They thought that they would be perfectly happy if they only had a king. A stork was sent to rule over them. The frogs went out to meet him gladly. The stork put forth his head, took up a frog and swallowed him. Then the frogs were very sorry that they had asked for a king.

Every day the stork king did the same thing until all the poor frogs had disappeared.

Birthday: Lyman Abbott, a Congregational clergyman, author, and journalist, son of Jacob Abbott, born at Roxbury, Mass., December 18, 1835. Editor of *The Outlook*.

19 MANNERS

Do you wish the world were better?
  Let me tell you what to do.
Set a watch upon your actions,
  Keep them always straight and true.
Rid your mind of selfish motives,
  Let your thoughts be clean and high.
You can make a little Eden,
  Of the sphere you occupy.

A SERIES OF DON'TS

DON'T slight a boy because his home is plain and unpretending. Abraham Lincoln's home was a log cabin.

Don't slight a boy because of the ignorance of his parents. Shakespeare, the world's poet, was the son of a man who was unable to write his own name.

Don't slight a boy because he chooses an humble trade. The author of *Pilgrim's Progress* was a tinker.

Don't slight a boy because of physical disability. Milton was blind.

Don't slight a boy because of dullness in his lessons. Hogarth, the celebrated painter and engraver, was a stupid boy at his books.

Don't slight any one; not alone because some day they may far outstrip you in the race of life, but because it is neither right, nor kind, nor polite.—*Selected*

Read: *Nixie Bunny in Manners-Land*, by Sindelar, to the little folks; "The Knights and the Naughty Child," from Bakewell's *True Fairy Stories*.

Birthday: Edwin McMasters Stanton, an American lawyer and statesman, born at Steubenville, Ohio, December 19,
1814; died at Washington, D. C., December 20, 1869.

20 PURPOSE

I RESOLVE

To keep my health;
To do my work;
To live:
To see to it I grow and gain and give:
Never to look behind me for an hour:
To wait in weakness, and to walk in power:
But always fronting onward to the light:
Always and always facing toward the light.
—*Charlotte P. Stetson*

21 PERSEVERANCE

The great secret of success in life is for a man to
be ready when his opportunity comes.—*Disraeli*

INDUSTRY AND APPLICATION

Mr. Disraeli affords an instance of the power of industry and application in working out an eminent career.
His first achievements were, like Bulwer's, in literature;
and he reached success only through a succession of failures. As an orator, too, his first appearance in the House
of Commons was a failure. Though composed in a grand
and ambitious strain, every sentence was hailed with
"loud laughter." Yet he felt so sure that he would some
day be a great man that he ended by saying: "I have
begun several times many things, and have succeeded in
them at last. I will sit down now, but the time will come
when you will hear me." The time did come; and how
Disraeli succeeded affords a striking illustration of what
energy and determination will do.

Birthday: Benjamin Disraeli, earl of Beaconsfield, a
noted English writer and statesman, born in London, England, December 21, 1805; died on April 19, 1881.

22 HEROES

Here's to the boy who has courage to say
"No!" when he's tempted, and turn straight away
From temptation and tempter, and do what is right—
Such boys are heroes who'll win in the fight.

Here's to the boy who is willing to work,
And, if he could, not a duty would shirk;
Doing his best at his work or his play—
Such boys will do to depend on, I say.
—Hezekiah Butterworth

Sing: "When the Swallows Homeward Fly," by Franz Abt.

Birthdays: Franz Abt, a German composer, born at Eilenberg, Prussian Saxony, December 22, 1819; died at Weisbaden, April 2, 1885.

Hezekiah Butterworth, an American writer for young folks, born in Warren, R. I., December 22, 1839; died September 5, 1905.

23 CHRISTMAS
[December 25]

'Tis the time of the year for the open hand,
And the tender heart and true,
When a rift of heaven has cleft the skies
And the saints are looking through.
—Margaret Sangster

Read: "How Uncle Sam Observes Christmas," from *Our Holidays: Retold from St. Nicholas;* "Christmas Everywhere," by Phillips Brooks; "Christmas Like it Used to Be," by Nixon Waterman; "The First Christmas Tree," by Van Dyke.

Sing: Christmas songs from *Songs in Season.* Procure copy of Sindelar's *The Best Christmas Book* for other songs and entertainment material.

Birthdays: Hamilton Wright Mabie, an American author and critic, born at Cold Spring, N. Y., December 23, 1846; lives at Summit, N. J.

Harriet Monroe, an American author, born in Chicago, Ill., December 23, 1860; lives in Chicago.

24 CHRISTMAS
[Continued]

I heard the bells on Christmas Day,
Their old familiar carols play
    And wild and sweet
    The words repeat
Of peace on earth, good-will to men.
  *   *   *   *   *   *   *

Then pealed the bells more loud and deep;
God is not dead; nor doth he sleep!
    The wrong shall fail,
    The right prevail,
With peace on earth, good-will to men.
                    —Longfellow

Birthdays: William Makepeace Thackeray, a famous English writer, born at Calcutta, British India, July 18, 1811; died December 24, 1863.

Matthew Arnold, an English poet, born at Laleham, England, December 24, 1822; died April 15, 1888.

25 CHRISTMAS
[Concluded]

"What means that star," the shepherds said,
  "That brightens through the rocky glen?"
And angels answering overhead,
  Sang, "Peace on earth, good-will to men."
—From "A Christmas Carol" by James Russell Lowell

JESUS OF NAZARETH

THE following extract has been translated from the writings of the contemporary historians of the period of Pope Innocent VIII.

Publius Lentulus, in those days Governor of Judea, wrote the following message to the Senate and People of Rome:

"There appeared in these days a most virtuous man, by the name of Jesus Christ, who still lives among us, and is considered by the heathens a Prophet of Truth, but called by His own disciples the Son of God. He raises people from the dead, and cures diseases of all kinds. Being a man of tall and imposing stature, strongly inspiring veneration by His appearance, He instills both love and fear into the minds of those who see Him. His hair has the color of a fully ripened hazelnut, almost smooth down to the ears, slightly curly lower down, and of a more oriental shade as it falls in a wavy mass upon His shoulders. In accordance with the custom of the Nazarenes it is parted in the middle. His brow is very smooth and bears the imprint of frankness. His face is free from blemishes and wrinkles, beautiful, and with a pleasing, rosy complexion. The lines of the nose and mouth are immaculate, the beard is rather full, of a shade well in harmony with the color of His hair and not very long. His eyes are gray, clear and animated. His body is shapely and vigorous, and His arms and hands are well proportioned. When censuring, He inspires awe; when admonishing, He is kindly and prepossessing. His speech is moderate, full of wisdom and modest, but at the same time dignified. No one can recollect seeing Him laugh, but many have seen Him weep.''

Tell about Newton and the law of gravitation.

Birthdays: Samuel de Champlain, a noted French navigator, born at Brouage, France, in 1567; died in Quebec, Canada, December 25, 1635.

Sir Isaac Newton, a famous English philosopher and mathematician, born at Woolsthorpe, Lincolnshire, England, December 25, 1642; died at London, March 20, 1727.

Clara Barton, ''America's Florence Nightingale,'' and the first president of the Red Cross Society of America, born at Oxford, Mass., December 25, 1822; died in 1892. (See ''The Red Cross,'' October 26, this book.)

Edwin H. Blashfield, an American painter, born in New York City, December 25, 1848; has his studio in New York. Painted *Christmas Chimes,* etc.

26 HUMILITY

Full many a gem of purest ray serene,
  The dark, unfathomed caves of ocean bear;
Full many a flower is born to blush unseen,
  And waste its sweetness on the desert air.
                                    —*Gray*

THE POMPOUS YOUNG MAN

A STORY is told of a pompous young man who bustled into a great lawyer's office.

"This is Mr. Sheldon?" he said.

"Yes," responded the lawyer.

"Well, I'm Mr. Harvey of Harvey, Wright & Company."

"Take a chair, Mr. Harvey," said the lawyer.

"My father was a cousin of Senator Harvey and I—"

"Take two chairs, Mr. Harvey!"

"It is indeed a good thing to be well descended—but the glory belongs to one's ancestors," says Nathaniel Hawthorne. So, always remember while admiring your family tree that it is the tree you gaze upon—and "You" may be a little rotten apple that has fallen to the ground.

Read: "Gray's *Elegy of a Country Churchyard*.

Sing: "Abide with Me," from *American School Songs*.

Birthdays: Thomas Gray, an English poet, born in Cornhill, London, England, December 26, 1716; died in London, July 24, 1771.

George Dewey, an American admiral, born at Montpelier, Vt., December 26, 1837; lives in Washington, D. C.

27 HELPFULNESS

Do something for each other,
  Though small the help may be;
There's comfort oft in little things,
  Far more than others see.

Read: *Life of Pasteur,* by René Vallery Radot. Chapter 13 tells of the first vaccination against hydrophobia given to a boy of nine years.

Birthdays: Johann Kepler, a famous German astronomer, born in Würtemberg, Germany, December 27, 1571; died in Ratisbon, Germany, November 15, 1630.

Louis Pasteur, a noted French chemist and microscopist, born at Dole, Jura, France, December 27, 1822; died in Paris, September 28, 1895.

28 ACCOMPLISHMENT

Whenever a task is set for you,
Don't idly sit and view it,
Nor be content to wish it done,
Begin at once to do it.

PRESIDENT WILSON'S ADVICE TO BOYS

"I DARE say you think that schoolmasters are often a bit hard on you in requiring you to do things in order that you may pass the tests of the school, but I want to warn you that when you get out of the school you are going to have harder schoolmasters than you had before. For the world requires that we make good, no matter what happens, and the man that does things amounts to a great deal more than the man who wishes he had done things and who promises he will do things. The men I am sorry for are the men who stop to think that they have accomplished something before they stop at the grave itself. You have got to have your second wind in this world and keep it up until the last minute."

Birthday: Woodrow Wilson, an American educator and the twenty-eighth president of the United States, also the first president since the Civil War to come from the South, born in Staunton, Va., December 28, 1856.

29 THE VALUE OF THINGS

Work, and the health to do it, are the greatest blessings God gives to mankind.—*Pearley*

A DIAMOND OR A COAL

BY CHRISTINA G. ROSSETTI

A DIAMOND or a coal?
  A diamond, if you please;
Who cares about a clumsy coal
  Beneath the summer trees?

A diamond or a coal?
  A coal, sir, if you please;
One comes to care about the coal
  At times when waters freeze.

Birthdays: Andrew Johnson, seventeenth president of the United States, born in Raleigh, N. C., December 29, 1808; died near Elizabethtown, Tenn., July 31, 1875.

William E. Gladstone, a famous English statesman, called the "Great Commoner," born in Liverpool, England, December 29, 1809; died at his residence, Hawarden Castle, near Chester, May 19, 1898.

Christina Georgina Rossetti, an English poet of Italian origin, born in London, England, 1830; died December 29, 1894.

30 TRUST

God of our fathers, known of old—
  Lord of our far-flung battle line—
Beneath whose awful hand we hold
  Dominion over palm and pine—
Lord God of Hosts, be with us yet,
  Lest we forget—lest we forget.
              —*Rudyard Kipling*

THE VALUE OF A GOOD NAME

JUST as the Civil War commenced, soldiers were enlisting, and going away from almost every home in the land. A young man had volunteered, and was expecting daily to be ordered to the seat of war. One day his mother gave him an unpaid bill with the money, and asked him to pay it. When he returned home at night, she said, "Did you pay that bill, George?"—"Yes," he answered, "I paid it." In a few days the bill was sent in a second time. "I thought," said she to her son, "that you paid this."—"I really do not remember, mother; you know, I've so many things on my mind."—"But you said you paid it."—"Well," he answered, "if I said I paid it, I did."

He went away to his company, and his mother went herself to the store. "I am quite sure," she said to the merchant, "that my son paid this bill some days ago. He has been very busy since, and has quite forgotten about it, but he told me that he had paid it the day I gave him the money; and he says, if he said then that he had paid it, he is quite sure that he did."—"Well," said the merchant, "I forgot about it; but, if your son ever said he paid it, he did. I have known George all his life, and his word is as good with me as a receipt."

Read: "How the Camel Got His Hump," in *Just-So Stories,* by Kipling; "The Image and the Treasure," from Scudder's *Book of Legend;* "The Story of Truth," from Bakewell's *True Fairy Stories;* "The Stolen Corn," from Bailey and Lewis' *For the Children's Hour.*

Birthdays: George Gordon Meade, "The Victor of Gettysburg," born in Cadiz, Spain, where his father at the time was United States consul, December 30, 1815; died in Philadelphia, Pa., November 6, 1872.

Rudyard Kipling, an English writer of stories, novels, and poems, born in Bombay, India, December 30, 1865.

31 NEW YEAR'S EVE

Ring out, wild bells, to the wild sky
The flying cloud, the frosty light:
The year is dying in the night;
Ring out, wild bells, and let him die.

Ring out the old, ring in the new,
Ring, happy bells, across the snow:
The year is going, let him go;
Ring out the false, ring in the true.
—*From "In Memoriam," by Alfred Lord Tennyson.*

JANUARY

1 NEW YEAR'S DAY

Every day is a fresh beginning,
Every morn is the world made new,
.   .   .   .
Only the new days are our own;
To-day is ours and to-day alone.
—*Susan Coolidge*

NEW YEAR'S DAY CUSTOMS

THE custom of celebrating the first day of the year is a very ancient one. The exchange of gifts, the paying of calls, the making of good resolutions for the new year and feasting often characterize the day. The custom of ringing the church bells and the blowing of horns is of the widest extent.

The old-world custom of sitting up on New Year's night to see the old year out is still very common.

Read: "A Chinese New Year's in California," from *Our Holidays: Retold from St. Nicholas;* "Paul Revere's Ride," by Longfellow.

Sing: "January," from *Songs in Season.*

Birthdays: Edmund Burke, a famous British statesman and writer, born in Dublin, Ireland, January 1, 1730; died at Beaconsfield, England, July 9, 1797.

Paul Revere, an American patriot, born in Boston, Mass., January 1, 1735; died in Boston, May 10, 1818.

Anthony Wayne, an American general in the Revolution, born at Waynesborough, Pa., January 1, 1745; died in Presque Isle, December 14, 1796.

2 WHAT SHALL THE NEW YEAR BE?

A glad New Year or a sad New Year;
  O what shall the New Year be?
I cannot tell what it hath in store,
  I would that I might foresee;
But God knows well and I need no more;
  Is that not enough for me?
—*Selected*

Read: "New Year's Message," from Proudfoot's *Child's Christ Tales*.

Birthday: James Wolfe, an English general, born at Westerham, Kent, England, January 2, 1726; died September 13, 1759.

3 FAITHFUL TO TRUST

To thine own self be true;
And it must follow as night the day,
Thou can'st not then be false to any man.
—*Shakespeare*

A CRUEL BOY ALMOST SURE TO MAKE A CRUEL MAN

THERE was once a boy who loved to give pain to everything that came in his way, over which he could gain any power. He would take eggs from the mourning robin, and torture the unfledged sparrow, cats and dogs, the peaceable cow and the faithful horse; he delighted to worry and distress. I do not like to tell you the many cruel things that he did. He was told that such things were wrong. An excellent lady with whom he lived used to warn and reprove him for his evil conduct—but he did not reform. When he grew up he became a soldier. He was never sorry to see men wounded, and blood running upon the earth. He became so wicked that he laid a plan to betray his country, and to sell it into the hands of the enemy. This is to be a traitor. But he was discovered and fled. He never dared to return to his native land, but lived despised and died miserably in a foreign clime. Such was the end of the cruel boy, who loved to give pain to animals. He was born at Norwich, Conn., and the beautiful city of his birth is ashamed of his memory. His name was Benedict Arnold.

—*The Spirit of Humanity*

Birthdays: Benedict Arnold, an American general and traitor, born in Norwich, Conn., January 3, 1740; died in London, England, June 14, 1801.

Larkin Goldsmith Mead, an American sculptor, born at Chesterfield, N. H., January 3, 1835; died in Florence, Italy, October 15, 1910.

4   WORK AND PLAY

Work while you work,
Play while you play,
That is the way
To be cheerful and gay.

Sing: "Work and Play," from Kellogg's *Best Primary Songs*.

5   IDLENESS

He is not only idle who does nothing, but he is idle who might be better employed.—*Socrates*

THE VOICE OF NATURE

AMONG the disciples of Hillel, the wise teacher of the sons of Israel, was one named Saboth, whom every kind of labor displeased, so that he gave himself up to idleness and sloth. Hillel was grieved for the youth, and resolved to reform him. To this end he conducted him out one day to the valley of Hinnon, near Jerusalem.

Here there was a large pool of stagnant water, full of reptiles and vermin, and covered with slimy weeds. When they reached the valley, Hillel laid aside his staff, and said: "Here we will rest from our journey." But the youth was astonished, and said: "What! master; by this loathsome swamp? Do you not perceive what a poisonous odor arises from it?"

"Thou art right, my son," answered the teacher. "This swamp is like the soul of the idler. Who would remain in its vicinity?" Thereupon Hillel conducted the youth to a desolate field, in which grew only thorns and thistles, which choked the corn, and the wholesome plants.

Then Hillel leaned upon his staff and said: "Behold, this field has a fruitful soil, to bring forth all things agreeable and useful! But it has been forgotten and neglected. So it now produces stinging thistles, and thorns, and poisonous plants; and among them nestle snakes and moles. Before thou sawest the *soul;* now recognize the *life* of the idler."—*Adapted*

Sing: "What Kind of Boys," from Kellogg's *Best Primary Songs.*

Special Day: Arbor Day in Florida. (See *Arbor Day,* April 19 and 20, this book.)

6 LOYALTY

To all the world I give my hand;
My heart I give my native land,
I seek her good, her glory;
I honor every nation's name,
Respect their fortune and their fame,
But love the land that bore me.
—*Selected*

JOAN OF ARC

JOAN OF ARC was the daughter of poor peasants and in her girlhood was a servant in a tavern. France was then at war with England and the whole country was in great trouble. Joan used to listen to the talk of the travelers, and think a great deal about the misfortunes of her country. She longed to do something to help the king, and by and by she fancied that she had visions from heaven, and heard voices telling her that she must save the nation. This idea took such hold of her that at last she made the people believe that God had really sent her to do a great work. The king, Charles VII, consented to let her lead the soldiers in an attack upon the English at the siege of Orleans; and she did it so well that the English were beaten and driven out of the town.

After Charles was crowned at Rheims, Joan wanted to go home, for she thought her work was ended. But there were more battles to fight, and everybody now believed that wherever she went she would bring victory for the French army. So they would not let her go; and in the end poor Joan was taken prisoner by the enemy, after an unsuccessful battle, and burnt for a witch in the marketplace of Rouen, May 31, 1431. All the world has honored her since her death, and statues have been raised to her memory.

Birthdays: Joan of Arc (French: Jeanne d'Arc), called also the "Maid of Orleans," born at Domremy, Lorraine, France, January 6, 1412; burnt for a witch in the marketplace of Rouen, France, May 31, 1431.

Charles Sumner, an American statesman, born in Boston, Mass., January 6, 1811; died in Washington, D. C., March 11, 1874.

7 PATRIOTISM

Let little hands bring blossoms sweet,
  To brave men lying low;
Let little hearts to soldiers dead
  Their love and honor show.
We'll love the flag they loved so well,
  The dear old banner bright,
We'll love the land for which they fell,
  With soul, and strength, and might!
—S. M. Kneil

Learn: "A Salute to the Flag," by Charles Sumner.
Read: Whittier's "Barbara Frietchie." Tell the story

of the Battle of Bunker Hill and of Putnam's part in it.

Sing: "Proud Flag of the Free," from *Uncle Sam's School Songs.*

Birthdays: Israel Putnam, an American general, born at Salem, Mass., January 7, 1718; died at Brooklyn, Conn., May 19, 1790.

Millard Fillmore, thirteenth president of the United States, born in Cayuga Co., N. Y., January 7, 1800; died in Buffalo, N. Y., March 8, 1874.

8 CHEERFULNESS

Keep a smile on your lips: it is better
   To joyfully, hopefully try
For the end you would gain than to fetter
   Your life with a moan and a sigh.
There are clouds in the firmament ever
   The beauty of heaven to mar,
Yet night so profound there is never
   But somewhere is shining a star.

Keep a song in your heart; it will lighten
   The duties that come to your hand;
Its music will graciously brighten
   The work that the builder has planned.
Its notes to the lives that are saddened
   May make them hopefully yearn,
And yours shall be wondrously gladdened
   By songs they shall sing in return.
                              —*Nixon Waterman*

Sing: "The Happy Farmer," from *Songs Every One Should Know.*

Birthdays: Robert Schumann, a German writer of music, born in Zwickan, Saxony, Germany, January 8, 1810; died near Bonn, Germany. July 29, 1856.

James Longstreet, a noted Confederate general in the Civil War, born in Edgefield, S. C., January 8, 1821; died near Gainesville, Ga., January 2, 1904.

Special Day: Anniversary of the Battle of New Orleans, celebrated in Louisiana.

9 PERSEVERANCE

In the lexicon of youth which fate reserves for a
bright manhood, there is no such word as fail.—*Lytton*

10 LOYALTY

Such is the patriot's boast, where'er we roam,
His first, best country ever is at home.
—*Goldsmith*

ETHAN ALLEN AND THE GREEN MOUNTAIN BOYS

ETHAN ALLEN was born in Litchfield, Conn., January 10,
1738. When a boy his parents emigrated to Salisbury,
where most of his youth was spent, and in 1765 he emigrated
to what was then called the "New Hampshire Grants,"
now the State of Vermont. This was then claimed by both
New Hampshire and New York, and the settlers there
formed themselves into a company called "Green Mountain
Boys," to protect their interests, and chose Ethan Allen
for their leader. Soon after the fight at Lexington (1775),
he marched against Fort Ticonderoga and captured it.

In September of the same year Allen was captured by
the British while on an expedition against Montreal, and
carried to England in irons. After being kept a prisoner
for two and one-half years, he was exchanged for a British
colonel. The English who admired his courage, tried to
bribe him to take their side. Once, in New York, an officer
told him that his faithfulness had won General Howe's
good opinion, and that if he would join King George's
army he would be given a good position, and would be rewarded after the war with large estates in Vermont or
Connecticut. Allen told him that he was so much obliged
to General Howe for his opinion that he would not lose it
by turning traitor. "As to the offer of lands," said he,
"that is much like a similar offer once made by Satan to
Christ of all the kingdoms of earth, when in fact the old
devil didn't own an acre."

Sing: "The Flag of Our Union, Forever!" from *Uncle Sam's School Songs.*

Birthday: Ethan Allen, an American officer in the Revolution, born in Litchfield, Conn., January 10, 1738; died near Colchester, Vt., February 13, 1789. Leader of the "Green Mountain Boys."

11 PATRIOTISM

Then conquer we must, for our cause it is just,
And this be our motto—*In God is our trust:*
And the star-spangled banner in triumph shall wave
O'er the land of the free, and the home of the brave.
—*From "The Star-Spangled Banner" by Francis Scott Key*

THE STAR-SPANGLED BANNER

To-day is the birthday of Francis Scott Key, the author of "The Star-Spangled Banner." This song of national and undying fame was written under conditions so thrilling as to inspire the author with graphic power. In was born of interest and patriotism during a conflict when the flag was in danger, and was written by Francis Scott Key, a young lawyer of Baltimore, during the war of 1812. Under a flag of truce he paid a visit to a British fleet off Baltimore, for the purpose of obtaining the release of a friend (Dr. Beans) who was being held prisoner. On the same day the bombardment of Fort McHenry began, and fearing he might reveal their plans, the British would not permit the visitor to return ashore. All through the night he remained upon deck with Dr. Beans and in the light of the bursting shells they could see the American flag still waving over the old fort. And when in the first rays of the dawn he still beheld the glorious banner waving from its accustomed place Francis Scott Key wrote that wonderful song, The Star-Spangled Banner, upon the back of a letter.

The attack on Baltimore had failed, and the next day Mr.

Key was permitted to return to the city. In his room at the hotel he finished and perfected the famous poem, which was first printed in a Baltimore newspaper.

Sing: "The Star-Spangled Banner."

Birthdays: Alexander Hamilton, a famous American statesman, born in the island of Nevis, West Indies, January 11, 1757; died at Weehawken, N. J., July 12, 1804.

Francis Scott Key, author of "The Star-Spangled Banner," born in Frederick County, Md., August 1, 1779; died in Baltimore, January 11, 1843.

Bayard Taylor, an American author, born at Kennett Square, Chester County, Pa., January 11, 1825; died in Berlin, Germany, December 19, 1878.

12 INDEPENDENCE

Let independence be our boast,
Ever mindful what it cost;
Ever grateful for the prize,
Let its altar reach the skies!
—*Joseph Hopkinson*

Learn: "The Declaration of Independence."

Sing: "America."

Birthdays: Charles Perrault, a French writer, born in Paris, January 12, 1628; died in Paris, May 16, 1703. Wrote *Cinderella, Bluebeard, Little Red Riding Hood, Puss in Boots, Hop o' My Thumb*, etc.

John Hancock, a noted American statesman, and the first signer of the Declaration of Independence, July 4, 1774, born in Quincy, Mass., January 12, 1737; died at Quincy, October 8, 1793.

Jack London, an American author, born in San Francisco, Cal., January 12, 1876; lives at Glen Ellen, Cal.

13 CHARACTER

Character, like porcelain, must be painted before it is glazed. There can be no change when it is burnt in.
—*Henry Ward Beecher*

CARVING A NAME
BY HORATIO ALGER

I WROTE my name upon the sand,
  And trusted it would stand for aye;
But soon, alas; the refluent sea
  Had washed my feeble lines away.

I carved my name upon the wood,
  And, after years, returned again;
I missed the shadow of the tree
  That stretched of old upon the plain.

To solid marble next my name
  I gave as a perpetual trust;
An earthquake rent it to its base,
  And now it lies o'erlaid with dust.

All these have failed. In wiser mood
  I turn and ask myself, "What then?
If I would have my name endure,
  I'll write it on the hearts of men.

" 'In characters of living light,
  From kindly words and actions wrought;
And these, beyond the reach of time,
  Shall live immortal as my thought.' "

Sing: "The Old Oaken Bucket," from *Songs Every One Should Know;* "My Old Kentucky Home" and "Swanee River," from *Uncle Sam's School Songs.*

Birthdays: Samuel Woodworth, an American writer, born in Scituate, Mass., January 13, 1785; died in New York City, December 9, 1842. Best known as the author of the song "The Old Oaken Bucket."

Stephen C. Foster, an American writer of songs, born in Pittsburgh, Pa., July 4, 1826; died in New York City, Jan-

uary 13, 1864. Composer of "My Old Kentucky Home,"
"Old Folks at Home," and many other popular songs.

Horatio Alger, an American writer, born at Revere,
Mass., January 13, 1834; died at Natick, Mass., July 18,
1899.

14 THE SNOW

The snow had begun in the gloaming,
And busily all the night
Had been heaping field and highway
With a silence deep and white.

Every pine, and fir and hemlock,
Wore ermine too dear for an earl,
And the poorest twig on the elm tree
Was ridged inch deep with pearl.
—*James Russell Lowell*

Sing: "The Silently Falling Snow," from Kellogg's
Best Primary Songs.

Birthday: Lewis Carroll, the pen-name of Rev. Charles
Lutwidge Dodgson, when he wrote for young folks, an English clergyman and writer, born in 1832; died January 14,
1898. Best known for his *Alice's Adventures in Wonder-
land.*

15 NOBLENESS

Be noble! and the nobleness that lies
In other men, sleeping but never dead,
Will rise in majesty to meet thine own.
—*Lowell*

Learn: "Nobility," by Alice Cary.

Read: Bible, Matt. 7: 24-27.

Sing: "Onward, Christian Soldiers," from *American
School Songs.*

16 HABIT

We sleep, but the loom of life never stops; and the
pattern which was weaving when the sun went down is
weaving when it comes up to-morrow.—*Beecher*

17 OPPORTUNITY

Lost time is never found again, and what we call time enough, always proves little enough.
—Benjamin Franklin

BENJAMIN FRANKLIN

BY T. W. HIGGINSON

ONE of the Americans who rendered the greatest services to the liberty of their country was Dr. Benjamin Franklin. He was born in Boston, January 17, 1706, and was the son of a poor tallow chandler. When a boy, he learned the printer's trade; at seventeen he left home, and established himself in Philadelphia.

He and a young partner began business with no capital, and felt very grateful to a friend whom they met in the street and who gave them a five-shilling job. Afterward they set up a newspaper, and published an almanac called "Poor Richard's Almanac," which had a great circulation. They also dealt in all sorts of small wares—rags, ink, soap, feathers, and coffee.

Franklin was a great reader, and a great student of science, and especially of electricity. He formed the theory that lightning and the electrical fluid are the same thing. This he said in a pamphlet, and some readers thought it a very absurd view. Then he resolved to prove it. He and his young son made a great kite of a silk handkerchief, fastened a piece of sharpened wire to the stick, and went out to fly the kite in a thunder-storm.

As the low thundercloud passed, the electric fluid came down the string of the kite. When Franklin touched a key that he had fastened to the string, his knuckles drew sparks from it, and proved that there was electricity there. This led him to invent the lightning rod, which is now in almost universal use. This discovery at once made him very famous in Europe, as well as in America.

He was afterward sent to England on a public mission, and remained there till the outbreak of the Revolution. Returning to America, he was one of the framers and signers of the Declaration of Independence. He was sent to France as ambassador, and aided in making the treaty with France which secured the independence of the American colonies.

He was a man of the greatest activity, public spirit, and wit. He exercised great influence in all public affairs, and founded more good institutions and benevolent enterprises than any other American of his time. His last public act was to sign a memorial to Congress in behalf of the Philadelphia Antislavery Society, of which he was president, asking the abolition of slavery.

He lived to the age of eighty-four, dying in 1790. The whole nation mourned when he died.

Birthday: Benjamin Franklin, a famous American philosopher and statesman, born in Boston, Mass., January 17, 1706; died in Philadelphia, Pa., April 17, 1790.

18 KEEPING YOUR WORD

One may live as a conqueror, a king, or magistrate; but he must die as a man.—*Webster*

BLUCHER AT WATERLOO

WHEN Blucher was hastening over bad roads to help Wellington at Waterloo; his troops faltered. "It can't be done!" said they.

"It must be done," was Blucher's reply. "I have promised to be there, *promised*, do you hear? You wouldn't have me break my word?" And it was done.

Read: Daniel Webster's "Bunker Hill Oration;" Bible, Matt. 13: 3-9.

Sing: "Uncle Sam's Wedding," from *Merry Melodies*.

Birthday: Daniel Webster, a famous American statesman, born in Salisbury (now Franklin), N. H., January 18, 1782; died at his farm in Marshfield, Mass., October 24, 1852.

19   EDUCATION

Every man must educate himself. His books and teacher are but helps; the work is his.—*Webster*

JAMES WATT

ABOUT one hundred and fifty years ago, a little boy who lived at Greenock, Scotland, and whose name was James Watt, sat one day looking at a kettle of boiling water, and holding a spoon against the steam that rushed out of the spout.

His aunt, thinking him idle, said, "James, is it not a great shame for you to waste your time playing with the kettle?" But James was really not idle. He was observing the power of steam.

James grew to be a great and good man, and he developed the steam engine which is so useful to us to-day. So, because he was a close observer, the little boy playing with the kettle has given us the steam engine which to-day propels great ships across the ocean, hauls long trains of passenger and freight cars quickly across the country, and turns the great wheels that drive the heavy machinery in our great factories and mills.

Read: "The Landing of the Pilgrims," by Felicia Hemans, and show in connection Boughton's pictures.

Birthdays: James Watt, the inventor or rather improver of the steam engine, born in Greenock, Scotland, January 19, 1736; died at Heathfield, near Birmingham, England, August 25, 1819.

Robert E. Lee, a famous American general, born in Virginia, January 19, 1807; died at Lexington, Va., October 12, 1870.

Sir Henry Bessemer, an English engineer and founder of Bessemer steel, born at Charlton, Hertfordshire, England, January 19, 1813.

George H. Boughton, an English painter, born in Norfolk, in 1834; died at Campden Hill, January 19, 1905.

David Starr Jordan, an American educator, born at Gainesville, N. Y., January 19, 1851; president of Leland Stanford Junior University, Palo Alto, California.

20 HONESTY

There is only one failure in life possible, and that is not to be true to the best one knows.—Farrar

Birthdays: Richard Henry Lee, a famous American statesman, born at Stratford, Westmoreland County, Va., January 20, 1732; died in Westmoreland County, June 19, 1794.

Robert Morris, an American statesman and a signer of the Declaration of Independence, born at Lancashire, England, January 20, 1734; died in Philadelphia, Pa., May 8, 1806.

Nathaniel Parker Willis, an American writer, born in Portland, Me., January 20, 1806; died at his place called "Idlewild," near Newburgh, N. Y., January 21, 1867.

21 FORGIVENESS

So are great deeds as natural to great men
As mean things are to small ones.
—George MacDonald

LOVE YOUR ENEMIES

Angry looks can do no good,
    And blows are dealt in blindness;
Words are better understood,
    If spoken but in kindness.

Simple love far more hath wrought,
  Although by childhood muttered,
Than all the battles ever fought,
  Or oaths that men have uttered.

Friendship oft would longer last,
  And quarrels be prevented,
If little words were let go past—
  Forgiven, not resented.

Foolish things are frowns and sneers,
  For angry thoughts reveal them;
Rather drown them all in tears,
  Than let another feel them.

Tell the story of the Prodigal Son, Bible, Matt. 18; read Matt. 5:44.

Sing: "The Lord My Shepherd Is," from *American School Songs.*

Birthdays: John C. Fremont, a noted American explorer and general, sometimes called the "Pathfinder," born in Savannah, Ga., January 21, 1813; died in New York City, July 13, 1890.

Thomas J. (Stonewall) Jackson, an American Confederate general, born in Clarksburg, Va., January 21, 1824; died near Fredericksburg, Va., May 10, 1863.

22   WISDOM

Reading maketh a full man; conference, a ready man; and writing, an exact man.—*Francis Bacon*

EXPERIENCE

A MULE, a fox, and a lion were out walking together. They found a big piece of meat. The lion said to the mule: "You may divide the meat; you always share it so well." The mule divided the meat into three equal pieces and gave a piece to each. The lion was so angry that he killed the mule. Then he told the fox to share the meat.

The fox gave all the meat to the lion. The lion was pleased.

"How did you learn to share so well?" asked he.

"The dead mule taught me how," said the fox.

Read: "Odin's Search for Wisdom," from Mabie's *Norse Stories.*

Birthdays: Francis Bacon, an English philosopher and statesman, born in London, England, January 22, 1561; died at Highgate, England, April 9, 1626. Called by Pope, the poet "The wisest, brightest, meanest of mankind."

Gotthold Ephraim Lessing, a noted German writer, born in Saxony, Germany, January 22, 1729; died in Brunswick, Germany, February 15, 1781.

George Gordon (Lord) Byron, a famous English poet, born in London, England, January 22, 1788; died at Missolonghi, Greece, April 19, 1824.

23 LOVE AND TRUTH

He liveth long, who liveth well,
   All else is life but flung away;
He liveth longest who can tell
   Of true things truly done each day.

24 PERSISTENCE

Many strokes, though with a little ax,
Hew down and fell the hardest timbered oaks.
                    ·   —*Shakespeare*

Birthdays: Charles H. Niehaus, an American sculptor, born in Cincinnati, Ohio, January 24, 1855; lives in New York City.

Beatrice Harraden, an English novelist, born at Hampstead, England, January 24, 1864; lives in London, England.

25 PLEASURES

Pleasures are like poppies spread;
You seize the flower, the bloom is shed;
Or like the snowflake in the river,
A moment white, then lost forever.
        —*Robert Burns*

ADVICE OF ROBBY BURNS' FATHER

In Robert Burns' own words, this is the advice which his father gave him and which he never forgot:
He bade me act a manly part, though I had ne'er a farthing,
For without an honest manly heart no man was worth regarding.

Read: "To a Field Mouse" and "For A' That," by Robert Burns. A short biography of Burns will be found in the *New Era Fifth Reader*.

Sing: "Auld Lang Syne" and "Flow Gently, Sweet Afton," from Hanson's *Gems of Song*.

Birthdays: Robert Burns, the national poet of Scotland, born near Ayr, Scotland, January 25, 1759; died at Dumfries, Scotland, July 21, 1796.

Louise de la Ramée (Ouida), an English novelist, born at Bury St. Edmunds, Suffolk, England, in 1839; died at Villareggio, Italy, January 25, 1908.

26 REMEMBRANCE

There is a pretty little flower,
    Of sky-blue tint and white,
That glitters in the sunshine
    And goes to sleep at night.
'Tis a token of remembrance,
    And a pretty name it's got;
Would you know it if I told you?
    'Tis the sweet Forget-me-not.

27 MUSIC

Music hath charms to sooth a savage breast,
To soften rocks, or bend a knotted oak.
        —*Congreve*

A BOY WHO BECAME FAMOUS

A BOY only six years old was sailing with his father down the Danube. All day long they had been sailing past crumbling ruins, frowning castles, cloisters hidden away among the crags, towering cliffs, quiet villages nestled in sunny valleys, and here and there a deep gorge that opened back from the gliding river. They stopped at night at a cloister, and the father took little Wolfgang into the chapel to see the organ. It was the first large organ he had ever seen, and his face lit up with delight, and every motion and attitude of his figure expressed a wondering reverence.

"Father," said the boy, "let me play." Well pleased, the father complied. Then Wolfgang pushed aside the stool, and, when his father had filled the great bellows, the elfin organist stood upon the pedals. How the deep tones woke the somber stillness of the old church! The organ seemed some great, uncouth creature roaring for very joy at the caresses of the marvelous child.

The monks, eating their supper in the refectory, heard it, and dropped knife and fork in astonishment. The organist of the brotherhood was among them, but never had he played with such power. They listened; some crossed themselves; till the prior rose up and hastened into the chapel. The others followed; but when they looked up into the organ-loft, lo! there was no organist to be seen, though the deep tones still massed themselves in new harmonies, and made the stone arches thrill with their power.

"It is the devil!" cried one of the monks, drawing closer to his companions, and giving a scared look over his shoulder at the darkness of the aisle. "It is a miracle!" said another. But when the boldest of them mounted the stairs to the organ-loft, he stood as if petrified with amazement. There was the tiny figure treading from pedal to pedal, and at the same time clutching at the keys above with his little hands. He heard nothing, saw nothing, besides; his eyes beamed, and his whole face was lighted up with joy. Louder and fuller rose the harmonies, streaming forth in swelling billows, till at last they seemed to reach a sunny shore on which they broke; and then a whispering ripple of faintest melody lingered a moment in the air, like the last murmur of a wind harp, and all was still.

The boy was Wolfgang Mozart.

Birthday: Wolfgang Amadeus Mozart, a famous German writer of music, born in Salzburg, Austria, January 27, 1756; died in Vienna, Austria, December 5, 1791.

28 KINDNESS

Be kind and gentle to those who are old,
For kindness is dearer and better than gold.

WELLINGTON AND THE TOAD

THE Duke of Wellington was a very kind man. Once when walking in his garden he saw a boy playing with a toad. "What are you doing?" he asked.

"I am feeding my toad," said the boy. "My father is going to send me to school, and I am afraid my toad will die."

"Go to school, my boy," said the duke, "and I will take care of your toad."

He afterward wrote to the boy at school, to tell him that the toad was quite well.

Read: "The Grateful Foxes," from Cooke's *Nature Myths and Stories;* Bible, Matt. 7: 12.

Sing: "Speak Softly, Gently," from Hanson's *Gems of Song.*

Birthdays: Elizabeth Stuart Phelps Ward, an American writer, born at Andover, Mass., August 13, 1844; died in Newton Center, Mass., January 28, 1911.

Samuel Chester Reid, an American naval officer, born in

Norwich, Conn., August 25, 1773; died in New York City, January 28, 1861. (In 1818 Captain Reid suggested the present plan of the United States flag, with thirteen stripes instead of fifteen, and an additional star for each new state. In 1859 Congress passed a vote of thanks to him as the designer of the flag.)

29 CHARACTER

Character is what God and the angels know of us;
reputation is what men and women think of us.
—*Horace Mann*

Birthdays: William McKinley, twenty-fifth president of the United States, born at Niles, Ohio, January 29, 1844; shot by an assassin in Buffalo, N. Y., September 6 and died September 14, 1901.

Henry Lee (Light Horse Harry, as he was called and the father of Gen. Robert E. Lee), a noted American general, born in Virginia, January 29, 1756; died at Cumberland Island, Ga., March 25, 1818. (When Washington died Henry Lee was chosen by Congress to write an eulogy on him; in it occur the famous words, "First in war, first in peace, and first in the hearts of his countrymen.")

30 GOLDEN DEEDS

As one lamp lights another nor grows less,
So nobleness enkindleth nobleness.
—*From "Yussouf," by Lowell*

INFLUENCE OF GOOD DEEDS AND WORDS

BY CHARLES MACKAY

A TRAVELER through a dusty road,
  Strewed acorns on the lea;
And one took root and sprouted up,
  And grew into a tree.
Love sought its shade, at evening time,

To breathe its early vows;
And Age was pleased, in heats of noon,
To bask beneath its boughs:
The dormouse loved its dangling twigs,
The birds sweet music bore;
It stood, a glory in its place,
A blessing evermore!

A little spring had lost its way
Amid the grass and fern,
A passing stranger scooped a well,
Where weary men might turn;
He walled it in, and hung with care
A ladle at the brink;
He thought not of the deed he did,
But judged that toil might drink.
He passed again,—and, lo! the well,
By summers never dried,
Had cooled ten thousand parching tongues,
And saved a life beside!

A dreamer dropped a random thought,
'Twas old, and yet was new,
A simple fancy of the brain,
But strong in being true;
It shone upon a genial mind,
And, lo! its light became
A lamp of life, a beacon ray,
A monitory flame:
The thought was small; its issue great,
A watch-fire on the hill;
It sheds its radiance far adown,
And cheers the valley still!

A nameless man amid a crowd
That thronged the daily mart,

Let fall a word of Hope and Love,
    Unstudied from the heart;
A whisper on the tumult thrown,—
    A transitory breath,—
It raised a brother from the dust,
    It saved a soul from death.
O germ! O fount! O word of love!
    O thought at random cast!
Ye were but *little,* at the first,
    But *mighty,* at the last!

31 LIBRARY DAY

We should make the same use of books that the bee does of a flower; he gathers sweets from it, but does not injure it.

A LITTLE GIRL'S IDEAL PARTY

BY ISABEL YEOMANS BROWN

I'D LIKE to give a party some lovely summer day,
When the air is warm and fragrant with the scent of new-
    mown hay,
When song-birds warbling blithely and brooklets running
    free
And busy little insects all join in minstrelsy.

And who would be invited? First, that thoughtful little boy
With the heart so sweet and loving—I mean Lord Faunt-
    leroy;
Juanita and her brother; kind little Sara Crewe,
And Dorothy and Donald and a host of others too.

Yes, all the story people—"Little Women," "Little Men;"
And all Miss Alcott's people—the children of her pen.
And when it came to parting I'm sure we'd all agree
We had ne'er before attended such a pleasant company.

Read: "The Book," in Forman's *Stories of Useful Inventions;* "The First Printer" in Baldwin's *Thirty More Famous Stories Retold;* "The Printing Press," in Mowry's *American Inventions and Inventors.*

Sing: "Come, Come, Come," from Kellogg's *Best Primary Songs;* "Let's Higher Climb," from *Uncle Sam's School Songs.*

Birthdays: Franz Schubert, a celebrated German musician, born near Vienna, Austria, January 31, 1797; died November 19, 1828.

James G. Blaine, an American statesman; born at West Brownsville, Pa., January 31, 1830; died January 27, 1893.

FEBRUARY

1 KNOWLEDGE

If we do not plant knowledge when young, it will give us no shade when we are old.—*Lord Chesterfield*

HOW ABRAHAM LINCOLN TAUGHT HIMSELF

WHEN Abraham Lincoln was young he had not the chance which the boys and girls of to-day have of attending school. But he was very anxious to learn, and wherever he was, at every chance he could get, he was reading or studying.

In the winter evenings he sat in the chimney-corner and ciphered on the wooden fire-shovel, by the light of the blazing logs. When the shovel was covered with figures, he would shave them off with his father's knife and begin again.

"He read every book he could lay hands on," said his step-mother; and when he came across a passage that struck him, he would write it on boards, if he had no paper, and keep it there until he was so fortunate as to get some paper. Then he would look at it, write it, and repeat it until he committed it to memory.

Birthday: David Porter, an American naval commander, born in Boston, Mass., February 1, 1780; died in Constantinople, Turkey, March 28, 1843.

2 A WONDERFUL WEAVER

There's a wonderful weaver
High up in the air,
And he weaves a white mantle
For cold earth to wear.

With the wind for his shuttle,
The cloud for his loom,
How he weaves, how he weaves,
In the light, in the gloom.
—*From "A Wonderful Weaver," by George Cooper*

3 COMPANY

Birds of a feather flock together.—*R. Burton*

BAD COMPANY

A FARMER'S corn was destroyed by cranes that fed in his field. Greatly annoyed, he declared that he would find a way out of the trouble. A net was set in which the cranes were snared. There was also a beautiful stork among them who had been visiting with the cranes, and had come to them from a neighboring roof.

"Spare me," pleaded the stork. "I am innocent; indeed I am. I never touched any of your belongings."

"That may be true," answered the farmer; "but I find you among thieves and I judge you accordingly."

The only safe way is to keep out of bad company.

Read: "Good and Bad Apples," from Scudder's *Stories From My Attic.*

Birthdays: Albert Sidney Johnston, an American soldier, born at Washington, Ky., February 3, 1803; killed at the battle of Shiloh, April 6, 1862.

Joseph Eccleston Johnston, an American general, born in Prince Edward County, Va., February 3, 1807; died in Washington, D. C., March 21, 1891.

Felix Mendelssohn, a famous German musician, born in Hamburg, Germany, February 3, 1809; died in Leipsic, Germany, November 4, 1847.

Horace Greeley, a noted American writer, born at Amherst, N. H., February 3, 1811; died November 29, 1872.

Special Day: Arbor Day in Arizona (Friday following first day of February or April). (See *Arbor Day,* April 19 and 20, this book.)

4 COURTESY

To be polite is to do and say
The kindest things in the kindest way.

THE READY ANSWER

A very wealthy man, arriving in Boston, was met by a dirty-faced boy, who was shouting: "Morning paper, two cents!"

The man bought a paper and gave the boy in payment a five-cent piece. While the boy was getting the change, the man said, "Keep the three cents and buy a cake of soap with which to wash your face."

The boy had by this time found the money, which he handed to the man, saying: "Take the money and buy a book on politeness."

The man was very much ashamed of himself and hurried away, while those near by smiled at the boy's ready answer.

Read: "For the Little Boy Who Will Not Say Please," from Burt's *Stories from Plato.*

5 PERSEVERANCE

The fisher who draws in his net too soon
Won't have any fish to sell;
The child who shuts up his book too soon
Won't learn any lessons well.

—*Ibid*

Read: "Bernard of Tuileries" and "A Tribune of the People," from Marden's *Stories from Life;* Bible, Luke 9: 62.

Sing: "In Life's Morning," from *School Song Knapsack.*

Birthdays: Ole Borneman Bull, a noted Norwegian violinist, born at Bergen, Norway, February 5, 1810; died August 17, 1880.

Dwight Lyman Moody, an American revival preacher,

born at Northfield, Mass., February 5, 1837; died at East Northfield, December 22, 1899.

6 COURAGE

I dare do all that may become a man; who dares do
more is none.—*Shakespeare*

TEN THINGS TO REMEMBER

THERE are ten things for which no one has ever yet been sorry. These are: For doing good to all; for speaking evil of none; for hearing before judging; for thinking before speaking; for holding an angry tongue; for being kind to the distressed; for asking pardon for all wrongs; for being patient towards everybody; for stopping the ears to a talebearer; for disbelieving most of the ill reports.

—*Selected*

Birthday: Sir Henry Irving, a noted English actor, born at Keinton, England, February 6, 1838; died at Bradford, England, October 13, 1905. [His real name was John Henry Brodribb.]

7 SUCCESS

It is when our budding hopes are nipped beyond recovery by some rough wind, that we are the most
disposed to picture to ourselves what flowers they might
have borne if they had flourished.—*Dickens*

"WHATEVER IS WORTH DOING"

ONCE when Charles Dickens was asked for the secret of his success, he replied that it was due to hard work and a motto which he had faithfully tried to live up to: "Whatever is worth doing is worth doing well." His son said of him: "Whatever he did, he put his whole heart into, and did as well as he could. Whether it was for work or for play, he was always in earnest." One of Dickens' sayings was: "Boys, do all the good you can, and don't make any fuss about it."

Read: Dickens' *David Copperfield*, which is almost the true story of Dickens' own life; *Pickwick Papers; Oliver Twist; Nicholas Nickleby; The Old Curiosity Shop; A Christmas Carol;* also "Dickens in Camp," by Bret Harte.

Birthday: Charles Dickens, a famous English writer of novels and one of the world's greatest story-tellers, born at Landport, England, February 7, 1812; died at his home, called Gadshill, near Rochester, England, June 9, 1870.

8 WORTH

A thing is worth precisely what it can do for you,
not what you choose to pay for it.—*Ruskin*

Read: Ruskin's *The King of the Golden River.*

Birthdays: John Ruskin, a famous English art critic and author, born in London, England, February 8, 1819; died at Brantwood, England, January 20, 1900.

William Tecumseh Sherman, an American general, born at Lancaster, Ohio, February 8, 1820; died in New York City, February 14, 1891.

Richard Watson Gilder, an American poet, born at Bordentown, N. J., February 8, 1844; died November 18, 1909.

9 WORK

The genius of success is still the genius of labor.
—*Garfield*

A DAWNING DAY

BY THOMAS CARLYLE

So here hath been dawning
Another blue day.
Think! Wilt thou let it
Slip useless away?

Out of Eternity
This new day is born;
Into Eternity
At night doth return.

Behold it beforehand
No eye ever did;
So soon it forever
From all eyes is hid.

Here hath been dawning
Another blue day.
Think! wilt thou let it
Slip useless away?

Read: "Training for Greatness," from Marden's *Stories from Life.*

Sing: "The Work of the Week," from *Songs in Season.*

Birthdays: William Henry Harrison, ninth president of the United States, born in Berkeley, Va., February 9, 1773; died in Washington, D. C., just one month after taking the oath of office, April 4, 1841.

George Ade, an American author and playwright, born in Kentland, Ind., February 9, 1866; living at Hazelden Farm, Brook, Ind.

Paul Laurence Dunbar, an American poet of African descent, born at Dayton, Ohio, June 27, 1872; died at Dunbar, Ohio, February 9, 1906.

Special Day: Arbor Day in Louisiana. (See *Arbor Day,* April 19 and 20, this book.)

10 GOODNESS

The plainest face has beauty,
    If the owner's kind and true;
And that's the kind of beauty
    My boy and girl, for you.

"THE HANDSOMEST MAN I EVER SAW"

AMONG the many stories told of President Lincoln the following deserves a worthy place: Hon. Thaddeus Stevens called with an elderly lady in great trouble, whose son had been in the army, but for some offense had been court-martialed and sentenced either to death or imprisonment. After a full hearing, the President proceeded to execute the paper granting pardon. The gratitude of the mother was too deep for expression, save by her tears, and not a word was said between her and Mr. Stevens until they were half way down the stairs when she suddenly broke forth in an excited manner with the words, "I knew it was a copperhead lie!" "What do you refer to, madam?" asked Mr. Stevens. "Why, they told me he was an ugly-looking man," she replied, with vehemence. "He is the handsomest man I ever saw in my life!"

11 PERSEVERANCE

Strongest minds
Are often those of whom the noisy world
Hears least. —*Wordsworth*

THE STORY OF EDISON

THOMAS A. EDISON was born a poor boy. He received but little education, and when quite young became a news-boy on a railroad train. Becoming interested in chemistry, he fitted up a small laboratory in one of the cars, where he tried experiments; but one day he came near setting fire to the train, and as a consequence he and his whole outfit were kicked out by the conductor. He then got some old type and began printing a little newspaper of his own, which he sold on the trains.

Having become acquainted with the telegraph operators along the line, he learned how to telegraph, and got a place in a telegraph office. Here again he tried so many experiments and attempted so many things thought to be im-

possible, that he soon got the name of "Looney" (for luna-
tic) and lost his situation. This did not discourage him,
and he became so skillful an operator that he was given
the best place in the telegraph office in Boston. After ex-
perimenting a long time Mr. Edison discovered a way of
sending several telegraphic messages at one time over the
same wires. He also made many improvements in the
telephone and in electric light; but his greatest invention
is the phonograph.

Read: Habberton's *Poor Boys' Chances;* Hamilton
Wright Mabie's *Men Who Have Risen;* Macomber's *Stories
of Great Inventors.*

Sing: "Work, for the Night is Coming," from *American
School Songs.*

Birthdays: Daniel Boone, an American hunter and
pioneer, born in Bucks County, Pa., February 11, 1735;
died in Missouri, September 26, 1820.

Thomas A. Edison, an American inventor, born in Milan,
Ohio, February 11, 1847; lives at Llewellyn Park, West
Orange, N. J.

12 ABRAHAM LINCOLN

Great captains, with their guns and drums,
  Disturb our judgment for the hour,
But at last silence comes;
  These all are gone, and, standing like a tower,
Our children shall behold his fame:
  The kindly-earnest, brave, foreseeing man,
Sagacious, patient, dreading praise, not blame,
  New birth of our new soil, the first American.
                          —*James Russell Lowell*

THE SOLDIER'S REPRIEVE

MRS. R. D. C. ROBBINS

PART I

"I THOUGHT, Mr. Allan, when I gave my Bennie to his
country, that not a father in all this broad land made so

precious a gift—no, not one. The dear boy only slept a minute, just one little minute, at his post. I know that was all, for Bennie never dozed over a duty. How prompt and reliable he was! I know he only slept one little second;—he was so young, and not strong, that boy of mine! Why, he was as tall as I, and only eighteen! And now they shoot him—because he was found asleep when doing sentinel-duty. 'Twenty-four hours,' the telegram said. Only twenty-four hours! Where is Bennie now?''

"We will hope, with his Heavenly Father," said Mr. Allan, soothingly.

"Yes, yes; let us hope. God is very merciful! 'I should be ashamed, father,' Bennie said, 'when I am a man, to think I never used this great right arm' (and he held it out so proudly before me) 'for my country, when it needed it. Palsy it, rather than keep it at the plow.' 'Go, then— go, my boy,' I said, 'and God keep you!' God has kept him, I think, Mr. Allan."

"Like the apple of his eye, Mr. Owen; doubt it not."

Little Blossom sat near them, listening, with blanched cheek. She had not shed a tear. Her anxiety had been so concealed that no one had noticed it. Now she answered a gentle tap at the kitchen door, opening it to receive a letter from a neighbor's hand. "It is from him," was all she said.

It was like a message from the dead! Mr. Owen took the letter, but could not break the envelope on account of his trembling fingers, and held it toward Mr. Allan, with the helplessness of a child.

The minister opened it, and read as follows:—

"DEAR FATHER: When this reaches you—I—shall—be in—eternity. At first it seemed awful to me; but I have thought about it so much now, that it has no terror. They say they will not bind me nor blind me, but that I may meet my death like a man. I thought, father, it might have been on the battlefield for my country, and that, when I fell, it would be fighting gloriously; but to be shot down like a dog for nearly betraying it—to die for neglect of duty!—oh, father, I wonder the very thought does not kill me! But I shall not disgrace you. I am going to write you all about it; and, when I am gone, you may tell my comrades. I can not now. You know I promised Jimmie Carr's mother I would look after her boy; and, when he fell sick, I did all I could for him. He was not strong when ordered back into the ranks, and the day before that night I carried all his luggage, besides my own, on our march. Toward night we went in on double-quick, and though the luggage began to feel very heavy, everybody else was tired too. And as for Jimmie, if I had not lent him an arm now and then, he would have dropped by the way. I was all tired out when we went into camp, and then it was Jimmie's turn to be sentry, and I would take his place; but I was too tired, father. I could not have kept awake if a gun had been pointed at my head; but I did not know it until—well—until it was too late."

"God be thanked!" said Mr. Owen. "I knew Bennie was not the boy to sleep carelessly at his post."

"They tell me, to-day, that I have a short reprieve—'time to write to you,' our good colonel says. Forgive him, father; he only does his duty; he would gladly save me if he could. And do not lay my death up against Jimmie. The poor boy is broken-hearted, and does nothing but beg and entreat them to let him die in my stead.

"I can't bear to think of mother and Blossom. Comfort them, father! Tell them I die as a brave boy should, and that, when the war is over, they will not be ashamed of me, as they must be now. God help me; it is very hard to bear! Good-by, father! God seems near and dear to me, as if he felt sorry for his poor, broken-hearted child, and would take me to be with him—in a better, better life.

"To-night I shall see the cows all coming home from

pasture, and precious little Blossom standing on the back stoop, waiting for me; but—I—shall never—never—come! God bless you all! Forgive your poor Bennie.''

PART II

Late that night a little figure glided down the foot-path toward the Mill Depot. The conductor, as he reached down to lift her into the car, wondered at the tear-stained face that was upturned toward the dim lantern he held in his hand.

A few questions and ready answers told him all; and no father could have cared more tenderly for his only child, than he for our little Blossom. She was on her way to Washington, to ask President Lincoln for her brother's life. She had brought Bennie's letter with her; no good, kind heart, like the President's, could refuse to be melted by it.

The next morning they reached New York, and the conductor hurried her on to Washington. Every minute, now, might be the means of saving her brother's life.

The President had but just seated himself to his evening's task, when the door softly opened, and Blossom, with downcast eyes and folded hands, stood before him.

''Well, my child,'' he said, in his pleasant, cheerful tones, ''what do you want?''

''Bennie's life, please, sir,'' faltered Blossom.

''Bennie! Who is Bennie?''

''My brother, sir. They are going to shoot him for sleeping at his post.''

''Oh, yes; I remember. It was a fatal sleep. You see, child, it was a time of special danger. Thousands of lives might have been lost by his negligence.''

''So my father said,'' replied Blossom, gravely. ''But poor Bennie was so tired, sir, and Jimmie so weak. He did the work of two, sir, and it was Jimmie's night, not his;

but Jimmie was too tired, and Bennie never thought about himself, that he was tired too.''

''What is this you say, child? Come here; I do not understand.'' And the kind man, as ever, caught eagerly at what seemed to be a justification of an offense.

Blossom went to him. He put his hand tenderly on her shoulder, and turned up the pale, anxious face toward his. How tall he seemed! And he was President of the United States, too! A dim thought of this kind passed for a moment through Blossom's mind; but she told her simple, straightforward story, and handed Bennie's letter to Mr. Lincoln to read.

He read it carefully; then, taking up his pen, wrote a few hasty lines and rang his bell. Blossom heard this order given: ''Send this dispatch at once.''

The President then turned to the girl, and said: ''Go home, my child, and tell that father of yours, who could approve his country's sentence, even when it took the life of a child like that, that Abraham Lincoln thinks the life far too precious to be lost. Go back, or—wait until to-morrow; Bennie will need a change after he has so bravely faced death; he shall go with you.''

''God bless you, sir!'' said Blossom.

Two days after this interview, the young soldier came to the White House with his little sister. He was called into the President's private room, and a strap fastened upon his shoulder. Mr. Lincoln then said: ''The soldier that could carry a sick comrade's baggage, and die for the act so uncomplainingly, deserves well of his country.''

Then Bennie and Blossom took their way to their Green-Mountain home. A crowd gathered at the Mill Depot to welcome them back; and, as Farmer Owen's hand grasped that of his boy, tears flowed down his cheeks, and he was heard to say fervently, ''The Lord be praised!''

Learn: ''The Gettysburg Address.''

Read: Speeches by Lincoln; "Abraham Lincoln," from *Our Holidays: Retold from St. Nicholas;* Arnold's *Life of Abraham Lincoln;* Baldwin's *Abraham Lincoln;* "Training for Greatness," in Marden's *Stories from Life.* *The Perfect Tribute,* by Andrews. For tributes in verse, songs, entertainment, etc., procure a copy of Sindelar's *Lincoln Day Entertainments.*

Sing: "Lincoln," from *Songs in Season,* and "America."

Birthdays: Cotton Mather, a famous New England divine and author, born in Boston, Mass., February 12, 1663; died in Boston, February 13, 1728.

Tadensz (Thaddeus) Kosciuszko, a Polish patriot, born near Novogrudek, in Lithuania, February 12, 1746; died in Solothurn, Switzerland, October 15, 1817. (Was aide-de-camp to General Washington, and served with honor until the end of the Revolution, when he went back to his native country.)

Abraham Lincoln, sixteenth president of the United States, born in Hardin County, Ky., February 12, 1809; shot by an assassin [John Wilkes Booth] at Ford's Theater, Washington, April 14, 1865, and died the following day.

Charles R. Darwin, an English writer on natural history, born in Shrewsbury, England, February 12, 1809; died at Down, Kent, England, April 19, 1882.

George Meredith, an English novelist and poet, born in Hampshire, England, February 12, 1828, died at Boxhill, Surrey, England, May 18, 1909.

13 ABRAHAM LINCOLN

[Continued]

My captain does not answer, his lips are pale and still;
My father does not feel my arm, he has no pulse nor will;
The ship is anchored safe and sound, its voyage closed and done;
From fearful trip, the victor ship comes in, with object won;

Exult, O shores; and ring, O bells!
But I, with mournful tread,
Walk the deck; my captain lies,
Fallen, cold, and dead.

—*Walt Whitman, 1865*

"HE BELONGS TO THE AGES"

LINCOLN, who was shot a little after ten o'clock in the evening, lingered, unconscious, until early the next morning. When his spirit passed away, Secretary Stanton was the first to break the silence by saying, "Now he belongs to the ages." The grief of the people for the Nation's hero was well-nigh universal.

Read: Anecdotes pertaining to Lincoln given elsewhere in this book. (See index.)

14 ST. VALENTINE'S DAY

Every joy that heart can hold
Be thine this day a thousandfold.

THE DAY

CUSTOM decrees that on this day the young shall exchange missives in which the love of the sender is told in verses, pictures and sentiment. No reason beyond a guess can be given to connect St. Valentine with these customs. He was a Christian martyr, about 270 A. D., while the practice of sending valentines had its origin in the heathen worship of Juno. It is Cupid's day, and no boy or girl needs any encouragement to make the most of it.—*Our Holidays*

Read: "Who Began It," from *Our Holidays: Retold from St. Nicholas.*
Sing: "Valentine Day," from *Songs in Season.*
Birthdays: Sir William Blackstone, author of a famous law-book called *Commentaries of the Laws of England,*

born in London, England, July 10, 1723; died February 14, 1780.

Winfield Scott Hancock, an American general, born in Montgomery County, Pa., February 14, 1824; died at Governor's Island, N. Y., February 9, 1886.

Special Day: St. Valentine's Day.

15   FRIENDS

On the choice of friends
Our good or evil name depends.
—*Gay*

Birthdays: Galileo, an Italian philosopher and mathematician, born at Pisa, Italy, February 15, 1564; died at Arcetri, near Florence, Italy, January 8, 1642.

Cyrus Hall McCormick, an American inventor, born at Walnut Grove, Va., February 15, 1809; died in Chicago, Ill., May 13, 1884.

16   PERSEVERANCE

Everything comes to him who waits—and hustles while he waits.

DON'T GIVE UP

BY PHŒBE CARY

If you've tried and have not won,
   Never stop for crying;
All that's great and good is done
   Just by patient trying.

Though young birds, in flying, fall,
   Still their wings grow stronger;
And the next time they can keep
   Up a little longer.

Though the sturdy oak has known
Many a blast that bowed her,
She has risen again, and grown
Loftier and prouder.

If by easy work you beat,
Who the more will prize you?
Gaining victory from defeat,
That's the test that tries you!

Birthday: Ernst H. Haeckel, a noted German naturalist,
born at Potsdam, Prussia, February 16, 1834.

17   A GOOD NAME

He who steals my purse steals trash,
But he that filches from me my good name
Robs me of that which not enriches him,
And makes me poor indeed.
—*Shakespeare*

18   DEVOTION

He prayeth well, who loveth well
Both man and bird and beast.
He prayeth best who loveth best
All things both great and small,
For the dear God who loveth us—
He made and loveth all.
—*From "Ancient Mariner" by Coleridge*

CHARLES AND MARY LAMB

No MAN was more sympathetic than Charles Lamb. He
led a brave life. His sister Mary had times when she lost
her reason, and at one of these times she actually killed her
own mother. Charles, who was at this time but twenty-
one years of age, resolved to sacrifice his life to his "poor,
dear, dearest sister," and voluntarily became her companion. He gave up all thoughts of home and society.
Under the strong influence of duty, he renounced the only

attachment he had ever formed. With an income of scarcely five hundred dollars a year, he trod the journey of life alone, fortified by his attachment for his sister. Neither pleasure nor toil ever diverted him from his purpose.

When released from the asylum, Mary devoted part of her time to the composition of the *Tales from Shakespeare*, and other works. When she felt a fit of insanity coming on, Charles would take her under his arm and together they would walk sadly across the fields to the asylum.

When she had recovered her reason, she went home again to her brother, who joyfully received her—treating her with the utmost tenderness. "God loves her," he said; "may we two never love each other less." Their affection continued for forty years, without a cloud, except such as arose from the fluctuations of her health.

Read: Selections from *Tales from Shakespeare*, by Charles and Mary Lamb; "Damon and Pythias," as given on p. 32 of this book.

Sing: "The Lord is My Shepherd," from *American School Songs*.

Birthday: Charles Lamb, a famous English writer, born in London, England, February 18, 1775; died in Edmonton, England, December 27, 1834.

19   DEEDS

A man of words and not of deeds
Is like a garden full of weeds.

Birthdays: Nikolaus Copernicus, a famous astronomer, born in Thorn, Poland, February 19, 1473; died at Frauenburg, Prussia, May 24, 1543.

Edgar Allen Poe, an American poet and story writer, born in Boston, Mass., February 19, 1809; died in Baltimore, Md., October 7, 1849.

Adeline Patti, a celebrated Italian opera singer, born in Madrid, Spain, February 19, 1843; lives in Wales.

20 INDUSTRY

Plow deep while sluggards sleep, and you'll have corn to sell and keep.—*Franklin*

THE IDLE LITTLE BOY

THERE was once an idle little boy. He did not know much. His mother sent him to school. He did not wish to go, so he went off to play.

He said, "How pretty the trees look! The sun shines and the birds sing. I will not go to school. I will play."

Soon he saw a bee. The bee flew from flower to flower. The little boy said, "Come and play with me."

But the bee said, "No, I must get some honey. I must not be idle." So he flew away.

Then the little boy met a dog. "Dog, will you play with me?" he said.

But the dog said, "I must not be idle. I must go and catch a rabbit."

Then the boy saw a bird. He said, "Birdie, come and play with me."

But the bird said, "I must make a nest." So the bird flew away.

Then a horse came along. "Horse, will you play with me?"

"No, I must go and plough the field. Then we can have some corn."

"Oh, dear! I will go to school. I can't play alone," said the boy. So off he went to school and learned his lessons.

—*Tweed's Supplementary Reader*

Birthdays: David Garrick, an English actor, born in Hereford, England, February 20, 1716; died in London, England, January 20, 1779.

Joseph Jefferson, a noted American actor, born in Philadelphia, Pa., February 20, 1829; died at Palm Beach, Fla., April 23, 1905.

21 PATRIOTISM

Oh, Washington! thou hero, patriot, sage,
Friend of all climes and pride of every age!
—*Thomas Paine*

THE VETERAN ARMY

DURING our Revolutionary War, eighty old German soldiers, who, after having long served under different monarchs in Europe, had retired to America and converted their swords into plowshares, voluntarily formed themselves into a company, and distinguished themselves in various actions in the cause of independence. The captain was nearly one hundred years old, had been in the army forty years, and present in seventeen battles. The drummer was ninety-four, and the youngest man in the corps on the verge of seventy.

Instead of a cockade, each man wore a piece of black crape, as a mark of sorrow for being obliged, at so advanced a period of life, to bear arms. "But," said the veterans, "we should be deficient in gratitude, if we did not act in defense of a country which has afforded us a generous asylum, and protected us from tyranny and oppression." Such a band of soldiers never before perhaps appeared on the field of battle.

Read: Bible, Psalm 136.

Sing: "Washington," from *American School Songs*.

Birthdays: John Henry Newman, an English cardinal and author, born in London, England, February 21, 1801; died at Edgbaston, England, August 11, 1890.

[James] Bradner Matthews, an American author, born in New Orleans, La., February 21, 1852; lives in New York City.

22 WASHINGTON'S BIRTHDAY

O Washington! thrice glorious name,
  What due rewards can man decree—
Empires are far below thy aim,
  And scepters have no charms for thee;
Virtue alone has your regard,
And she must be your great reward.
                            —*Philip Freneau*

THE INFLUENCE OF A GREAT NAME

WHEN Washington consented to act as commander-in-chief, it was felt as if the strength of the American forces had been more than doubled. Many years later, in 1798, when Washington, grown old, had withdrawn from public life and was living in retirement at Mount Vernon, and when it seemed probable that France would declare war against the United States, President Adams wrote to him, saying, "We must have your name, if you will permit us to use it; there will be more efficacy in it than in many an army." Such was the esteem in which the great President's noble character and eminent abilities were held by his countrymen!

Read: "Character of Washington," from *Cyr's Fifth Reader;* "Our Greatest Patriot," from Blaisdell and Ball's *Hero Tales from American History;* "The Boyhood of Washington," from *Our Holidays: Retold from St. Nicholas.* Use Sindelar's *Washington Day Entertainments* in preparing an entertainment program.

Sing: "Washington Song" and "The First Flag," from *Songs in Season;* "Mount Vernon Bells," from *School Song Knapsack.*

Birthdays: George Washington, "The Father of His Country" and first president of the United States, born in Westmoreland County, Va., February 22, 1732; died at Mt. Vernon, Va., December 14, 1799.

Jean Baptiste Camille Corot, a French landscape painter,

born in Paris, France, in July, 1796; died in Paris, February 22, 1875.

Sarah Flower Adams, an English poet, born at Great Harlow, County Essex, England, February 22, 1805; died in August, 1848. Author of "Nearer, My God, to Thee," etc.

James Russell Lowell, a famous American poet, born in Cambridge, Mass., February 22, 1819; died in Cambridge, Mass., August 12, 1891.

Special Days: Washington's Birthday; Lowell's Birthday; Arbor Day in Alabama and Texas. (See *Arbor Day*, April 19 and 20, this book.)

23 WASHINGTON'S RULES OF CONDUCT
[Found among his private papers after his death.]

Be no flatterer.

Mock not, nor jest at anything of importance.

Be not hasty to believe flying reports to the disparagement of any one.

Undertake not what you can not perform, but be careful to keep your promises.

Show not yourself glad at the misfortunes of another, though he were your enemy.

When a man does all he can though he succeed not well, blame not him that did it.

Labor to keep alive in your breast that little spark of celestial fire called conscience.

Whenever you reprove another be not blamable yourself for example is more prevalent than precept.

Associate yourself with men of good quality, if you esteem your own reputation, for it is better to be alone than in bad company.

Whisper not in the company of others.

Read no letters, books, or papers in company.

Every action in company ought to be some sign of respect to those present.

Come not near the books or writing of any one so as to read them unasked.

Speak not when others speak.

Speak no evil of the absent, for it is unjust.

Let your conversation be without malice or envy.

Be not apt to relate news if you know not the truth thereof.

Speak not in an unknown tongue in company, but in your own language.

Use no reproachful language against any one, neither
curse, nor revile.
When another speaks be attentive yourself, and disturb
not the audience.

Birthday: Sir Joshua Reynolds, a noted English portrait painter, born at Plympton, Devonshire, England, July
16, 1723; died in London, England, February 23, 1792.

24 WISDOM

Have more than thou showest
Speak less than thou knowest.
—*Shakespeare*

ROBERT FULTON

WHEN Fulton was building his steamboat, the Clermont,
everybody laughed at him. They thought he was wasting
his time and that a boat could not be run except by sails
or with an engine turned by men. But when the Clermont
was seen moving along on the Hudson River against both
wind and tide, the shores rang with shouts of delight, and
those who had jeered him were silent with wonder. In
1814 Fulton built for the United States the first steam
war-vessel ever made.

Sing: "Boat Song," from *Merry Melodies*.
Birthdays: Robert Fulton, a famous American inventor,
born at Little Britain, Lancaster County, Pa., in 1765;
died in New York City, February 24, 1815.
Winslow Homer, an American painter, born in Boston,
Mass., February 24, 1836; died at Scarboro, Me., September
29, 1910.

25 TIME

Lost, somewhere between sunrise and sunset, two
golden hours, each set with sixty diamond minutes.
No reward is offered for they are lost forever.
—*Horace Mann*

Birthday: Camille Flammarion, a French astronomer, born at Montigny-le-Roi, Haute-Marne, France, February 25, 1842.

26 PROGRESS

My idea is this: ever onward. If God had intended that man should go backward, he would have given him an eye in the back of his head.—*Victor Hugo*

Read: "The Good Bishop," from *Les Miserables,* by Victor Hugo, in Cabot's *Ethics for Children.*

Sing: "Sing, Smile, Slumber," from *Songs Every One Should Know.*

Birthday: Victor M. Hugo, a famous French poet and novel writer, born in Besancon, France, February 26, 1802; died in Paris, France, May 22, 1885.

27 LONGFELLOW'S BIRTHDAY

'Tis always morning somewhere, and above
The awakening continents, from shore to shore,
Somewhere the birds are singing evermore.
                              —*Longfellow*

Learn: Longfellow's "Excelsior," "The Legend Beautiful," "Robert of Sicily" and "The Psalm of Life."

Read: *The Story of Longfellow,* by Beebe; "Longfellow and the Children," from *Our Holidays: Retold from St. Nicholas;* selections from Longfellow's writings.

Sing: "Longfellow," from *Songs in Season;* "Stars of the Summer Night," from *Songs Every One Should Know;* "The Ship of State," "A Psalm of Life," and "Life is Real, Life is Earnest," from *Uncle Sam's School Songs.*

Birthday: Henry Wadsworth Longfellow, a famous American poet, born in Portland, Maine, February 27, 1807; died in Cambridge, Mass., March 24, 1882.

28   PATRIOTISM

Our band is few, but true and tried, our leader frank and bold:
The British soldier trembles when Marion's name is told.
Our fortress is the good greenwood, our tent the cypress tree:
We know the forest round us, as seamen know the sea;
We know its walls of thorny vines, its glades of reedy grass,
Its safe and silent islands within the dark morass.

—From "Song of Marion's Men," by Bryant

"THE SWAMP FOX"

GENERAL FRANCIS MARION was a daring and useful officer
in the Revolution. Sometimes he would fight with the army,
sometimes with bands of patriotic farmers and backwoods-
men on horseback, dashing through the country, surprising
the enemy at different points in the same day, then vanish-
ing as suddenly. The British were in constant dread of
"the Swamp Fox," as they called him. Marion and his
men lived in the swamps and forests, and had little food
or clothing. A British officer sent to ask an exchange of
prisoners, was led blindfolded into Marion's camp at Snow
Island. When their business was concluded Marion invited
the officer to dinner. To his utter astonishment, he saw
some roasted potatoes brought forward on a piece of bark,
of which the general partook freely and invited his guest
to do the same. "Surely, General," said the officer, "this
cannot be your ordinary fare!" "Indeed it is," replied
Marion, "and we are fortunate on this occasion, entertaining company, to have more than our usual allowance." It
is said that the young officer, on his return to Georgetown,
gave up his commission, declaring that such a people could
not be, and ought not to be, subdued.

Read: Bryant's "Song of Marion's Men;" Simms'
"Marion the Swamp Fox."

Francis Marion, "The Swamp Fox," an American general in the Revolution, born near Georgetown, S. Car., in
1732; died February 28, 1795.

MARCH

1 MARCH

O March that blusters, and March that blows,
What color under your footstep grows?
Beauty you summon from winter's snows
And you are the pathway that leads to the rose.
—*From "March," by Celia Thaxter*

Birthdays: Frederic Francois Chopin, a celebrated Polish composer and pianist, born near Warsaw, Poland, March 1, 1809; died in Paris, France, October 17, 1849.

William Dean Howells, an American novelist and poet, born in Martinsville, Ohio, March 1, 1837; resides in New York City.

2 WISDOM

True wisdom is to know what is best worth knowing,
and to do what is best worth doing.—*Humphreys*

THE STRANGE STORY OF SAM HOUSTON

WHEN Sam Houston was quite young he left home and went to live with the Cherokee Indians, one of whose chiefs adopted him for his son. He became noted as an Indian fighter, and fought bravely under General Jackson at the battle of Tallapoosa (March 24, 1814). In 1827 he was chosen governor of Tennessee, but resigned his office and went back to the Indians. In 1834 he went to Texas, then a part of Mexico, and when in 1835 the Texans began a war of independence he was made commander-in-chief of the army. He met the Mexican army under Santa Anna, the Mexican president, at the San Jacinto River, and though he had only half as many men Houston gained a splendid victory (April 21, 1836). The next day Santa Anna himself was captured, and forced to sign a treaty by which Texas was made independent. Houston was twice elected president of Texas, and ruled the country well and wisely. He made treaties with Indian tribes, brought back trade and peace with Mexico, and finally succeeded in having Texas admitted to the Union (1845). After that he was United States Senator and governor of Texas.

Sing: "Hail! Columbia," and "The Flag of the Union, Forever," from *Uncle Sam's School Songs.*

Birthdays: Sam Houston, an American soldier, born near Lexington, Va., March 2, 1793; died at Hunterville, Texas, July 25, 1863.

Carl Schurz, a German-American statesman and journalist, born near Cologne, Germany, March 2, 1829; died May 14, 1906.

Special Day: Anniversary of Texas independence, observed in Texas.

3 WORDS

Every gentle word you say,
One dark spirit drives away;
Every gentle deed you do,
One bright spirit brings to you.
—*V. B. Harrison*

HOW THE TELEPHONE WAS INVENTED

IN A recent lecture Prof. Alexander Graham Bell is reported to have explained, as follows, how he came to invent the telephone:

"My father invented a symbol by which deaf mutes could converse, and finally I invented an apparatus by which the vibrations of speech could be seen, and it turned out to be a telephone. It occurred to me to make a machine that would enable one to hear vibrations. I went to an aurist, and he advised me to take the human ear as my model. He supplied me with a dead man's ear, and with this ear I experimented, and upon applying the apparatus I found that the dead man's ear wrote down the vibrations.

"I arrived at the conclusion that if I could make iron vibrate on a dead man's ear, I could make an instrument more delicate which would cause those vibrations to be heard and understood. I thought if I placed a delicate piece of steel over an electric magnet I could get a vibration, and thus the telephone was completed. The telephone arose from my attempts to teach the deaf to speak. It arose from my knowledge, not of electricity, but as a teacher of the deaf. Had I been an electrician I would not have attempted it."

Birthday: Alexander Graham Bell, the inventor of the telephone, born in Edinburgh, Scotland, March 3, 1847; living in Washington, D. C.

4 INAUGURATION DAY

Always vote for a principle, though you vote alone, and you may cherish the sweet reflection that your vote is never lost.—*John Quincy Adams*

HOW THE DATE WAS SET

THE date of Inauguration Day was settled by the old Congress of the Confederation in 1788, when the procedure was established for the election of a President. It was decreed that the Electoral College should meet on the first Wednesday of January, the votes be counted by the House of Representatives on the first Wednesday of February, and the President be inaugurated the first Wednesday of March. The March date was the 4th. March 4 has been Inauguration Day ever since.   —*Our Holidays*

Read: "How a President Is Inaugurated," from *Our Holidays: Retold from St. Nicholas.*
Sing: "America."

Birthday: Count Casimir Pulaski, a Polish soldier, who fought in the American Revolution, born in Podolia, Poland, March 4, 1748; died at Savannah, Ga., October 11, 1779.
Special Day: Inauguration Day.

5 DUTY

Though your duty may be hard,
Look not on it as an ill;
If it be an honest task,
Do it with an honest will.
—*R. B. Sheridan*

Sing: "Duty and Inclination," from *Uncle Sam's School Songs.*

Birthdays: Antonio Allegri Correggio, a famous Italian painter, born at Correggio, now called Reggin, Italy, in 1494; died at Correggio, March 5, 1534.

Howard Pyle, an American artist and writer for young folks, born in Wilmington, Del., March 5, 1853; died in Florence, Italy, November 9, 1911.

6 BOOKS

Books are men of higher stature,
And the only men that speak aloud for
future times to hear!
—*Mrs. Browning*

MY BOOK IS A HOUSE

BY ABBIE FARWELL BROWN

It's a curious house, where people dwell,
And wonders happen, ill or well.
The door-plate gives the house's name,
Likewise the builder of the same.

You enter, if you have a key,
And something of a scholar be.
You ope the door, and in the hall
A picture greets you, first of all.

A blazoned notice next you view,
The builder's name, the owner's too,
The city where the house was made,
Date when the cornerstone was laid.

And then you find a list enrolled
Of treasures which the house doth hold,
That you may choose what suits your eye,
Or if none please may pass them by.

And then you swing door after door,
Each numbered next to that before,
From room to room you pass in turn,
And many curious things you learn

About the people of the house
(But you must keep still as a mouse).
A magic house, then, it must be,
For all things happen rapidly;

Behind its doors years pass away,
Though you may but an hour stay.
Perhaps around the world you soar
Before you pass the other door.

Yet when this gate is closed behind,
You have not stirred a step, you find!
Your hand may move the house at will,
Carry it far, or leave it still.

Though months and years may pass away,
Unchanged the house and inmates stay.
Your house to sell—or give—or let;
Yours to revisit or forget.

Read: "Sheridan's Ride," by Thomas Buchanan Read.

Sing: "The Old School-Bell," from *Uncle Sam's School Songs*.

Birthdays: Michael Angelo, a famous Italian painter, sculptor and architect, born near Florence, Italy, March 6, 1474; died in Rome, Italy, February 17, 1563.

Elizabeth Barrett Browning, wife of Robert Browning, a noted English poet, born at Coxhoe Hall, Durham, England, March 6, 1806; died June 30, 1861.

Philip H. Sheridan, an American general, born at Somerset, Ohio, March 6, 1831; died August 5, 1888.

7 BURBANK DAY

Flowers are cousins to children—
  So Frederick Froebel thought
When he planted the kindergarten,
  Where the children would be taught
To grow like the beautiful flowers,
  Under the gardener's care,
Removing the harsh and ugly,
  Keeping only the good and fair.
    —*Fannie F. Copeland*

"NATURE'S HELPER"

Luther Burbank when a boy cared but little for the regular school studies. He liked best to talk to the flowers, to study their ways, and to watch things grow. As he grew older he began to take a still greater interest in his "plant children," and to experiment with them in his endeavor to improve upon nature. Of course this seemed foolish to many people, but Mr. Burbank had an idea that he could do it and he was going to give it a trial. To-day we can see the results of Mr. Burbank's work in his new creations of flowers, fruits, plants and trees.

How many have seen the Burbank potato? the improved Shasta daisy? the white blackberry? the Burbank plum? the Burbank prune? But Mr. Burbank's greatest work is perhaps the improved fruit-bearing cactus. He has made it give up its thorns and its woody fibre, and grow instead a smooth outer covering, a rich juicy leaf and fruit that may be used for food. This cactus will make desert travel safe and will also furnish food for cattle on the vast areas that are annually visited by drouth.

Read or tell more of Mr. Burbank's life and work; Bible, Isaiah 35: 1, 6 and 7.

Sing: "Flower Day," from *Songs in Season;* "The Daisy," from *American School Songs.*

Birthdays: Sir Edwin Landseer, a famous English artist, born in London, England, March 7, 1802; died in London, October 1, 1873.

Luther Burbank, "nature's helper," born March 7, 1849; lives in Santa Rosa, California.

Special Day: Arbor Day in California. (See *Arbor Day,* April 19 and 20, this book.)

8 CLEANLINESS

Cleanliness of body was ever esteemed to proceed from a due reverence to God.—*Bacon*

CLEAN HANDS

A DERVISH of great sanctity one morning had the misfortune, as he took up a crystal cup which was consecrated to the Prophet, to let it fall on the ground, breaking it into pieces. His son coming in some time after, he stretched out his hand to bless him, as his manner was every morning; but the youth, going out, stumbled over the threshold and broke his arm. As the old man wondered at these events, a caravan passed by on its way to Mecca. The dervish approached it to beg a blessing; but, as he stroked one of the holy camels, he received a kick from the beast which sorely bruised him. His sorrow and amazement increased on him, until he recollected, that, through hurry and inadvertency, he had that morning come abroad without washing his hands.   —*Royal Series*

Birthday: John Ericsson, a famous engineer and inventor, born in the province of Wermeland, Sweden, July 31, 1803; died in New York City, March 8, 1889. (Inventor of the turret-ship Monitor, that defeated the Confederate ironclad ship Virginia, formerly the Merrimack, which was many times larger than the Monitor.)

9 SOWING AND REAPING

We can never be too careful
  What the seed our hands shall sow,
Love from love is sure to ripen,
  Hate from hate is sure to grow.
Seeds of good or ill we scatter
  Heedlessly along our way,
But a glad or grievous fruitage
  Waits us at the harvest day.
Whatsoe'er our sowing be,
  Reaping, we its fruit must see.

Sing: "Kind Words," from Kellogg's *Best Primary Songs;* "Sowing the Seed," from *American School Songs.*

Birthday: Franz Joseph Gall, a German physician, founder of Phrenology, born at Tiefenbrunn, near Pforzeim, Baden, Germany, March 9, 1758; died at Montrouge, near Paris, France, Aug. 22, 1828.

10 HONESTY

Whate'er you think, whate'er you do,
Whate'er you purpose or pursue,
It may be small, but must be **true.**

11 TRUST

I know not where His islands lift
  Their fronded palms in air:
I only know I cannot drift
  Beyond His love and care.
                        —*Whittier*

Read: Bible, Luke 12:22-30.
Sing: "Rock of Ages," from *Uncle Sam's School Songs.*

Special Day: Arbor Day in Oklahoma (second Monday in March). (See *Arbor Day,* April 19 and 20, this book.)

12 ACHIEVEMENT

Though the world smile on you blandly,
Let your friends be choice and few;
Choose your course, pursue it grandly,
And achieve what you pursue.

—*Read*

SALT IN YOUR CHARACTER

There is a loftier ambition than merely to stand high in the world. It is to stoop down and lift mankind a little higher. There is a nobler character than that which is merely incorruptible. It is the character which acts as an antidote and preventive of corruption. Fearlessly to speak the words which bear witness to righteousness and truth and purity; patiently to do the deeds which strengthen virtue and kindle hope in your fellow-men; generously to lend a hand to those who are trying to climb upward; faithfully to give your support and your personal help to the efforts which are making to elevate and purify the social life of the world,—that is what it means to have salt in your character. The men that have been happiest, and the men that are the best remembered, are the men that have done good.   —*Henry van Dyke*

Birthday: Thomas Buchanan Read, an American poet and artist, born in Chester County, Pa., March 12, 1822; died in New York City, May 11, 1872. Author of "Sheridan's Ride."

13 PATIENCE

Heaven is not gained by a single bound,
But we build the ladder by which we rise
From the lowly earth to the vaulted skies,
And we mount to its summit round by round.
—*J. G. Holland*

Read: "Diff'ent Kind o' Bundles,", from Slosson's *Story-tell Lib*.

Birthday: Benjamin Harrison, twenty-third president of the United States, born at North Bend, Ohio, August 20, 1833; died March 13, 1901.

14 HONOR

Where honor ceaseth, there knowledge decreaseth.
—*Shakespeare*

TRUE MANHOOD

It is not always the coat that tells,
Nor the collar your friend may wear;
It is not always the shine of the shoe,
Nor the finished touch of his hair.

It is not all in a silken hat,
Nor the fitting neat of his gloves;
It is not merely his cultured air,
Nor the circle in which he moves.

It is not his temper, his pride nor smile,
Nor yet his worshipful mien;
It is not even the name he bears
In a world that is shallow and mean.

Ah, no, after all, 'tis the man himself
As he stands with his God alone,
'Tis the heart that beats beneath the coat,
The life that points to the throne.

The eye that cheers with its kindly glance,
'Tis the arm 'round a brother cast;
The hand that points to a hope beyond,
'Tis a love that endures to the last.

Sing: "Help to Set the World Rejoicing," from *Uncle Sam's School Songs.*

Special Day: Arbor Day in New Mexico (second Friday in March). (See *Arbor Day,* April 19 and 20, this book.)

15 FAIR-MINDEDNESS

Do not look for wrong and evil;
  You will find them if you do;
As you measure for your neighbor,
  He will measure back to you.
  —*Alice Cary*

Birthday: Andrew Jackson, seventh president of the United States, born at Waxhaw Settlement, N. C., March 15, 1767; died at his farm called the Hermitage, near Nashville, Tenn., June 8, 1845.

16 HEALTH

Better than grandeur, better than gold,
Than rank or title a hundred-fold,
Is a healthy body, and a mind at ease,
And simple pleasures that always please.
A heart that can feel for a neighbor's woe,
And share in his joy with a friendly glow,
With sympathies large enough to infold
All men as brothers, is better than gold.
  —*Alexander Smart*

Read: "What Will You Choose," from Brown's *The House I Live In.*

Birthday: James Madison, fourth president of the United States, born at King George, Va., March 16, 1761; died at Montpelier, near Orange Court House, Va., June 28, 1836.

17 ST. PATRICK'S DAY

A very little seed of truth
  May sink into the soul,
And by God's blessing, gather power
  As ages onward roll.

ST. PATRICK AND THE SNAKES

A GREAT many stories are told of St. Patrick. In Ireland there are no snakes or other poisonous reptiles, and the people believe that the "Holy St. Patrick" charmed them all away. St. Patrick had destroyed all snakes, so runs the old legend, except one very large one who hid himself in the thick woods on the shores of the beautiful lake of Killarney. St. Patrick determined to catch him, so he procured a large chest with nine strong bolts, and taking it on his shoulder he trudged over to Killarney, where he found the snake basking in the sun. The snake was induced to enter the chest, and it was thrown into the lake. There to this day, it is said by the people about the lake, they can hear the voice of the snake crying: "Let me out; hasn't to-morrow come yet?"   —*Selected*

18   DESTINY

The tissues of the life to be
  We weave with colors all our own,
And in the field of destiny
  We reap as we have sown.
    —*Whittier*

Birthdays: Amerigo Vespucci, an Italian navigator, after whom America was named, born in Florence, Italy, March 18, 1452; died in Seville, Spain, February 22, 1512.

John C. Calhoun, an American statesman, born in the district of Abbeville, S. C., March 18, 1782; died at Washington, D. C., March 31, 1850.

Grover Cleveland, twenty-second and twenty-fourth president of the United States, born in Caldwell, N. J., March 18, 1837; died in Princeton, N. J., June 24, 1908.

19   CHARACTER

To form character is to form grooves in which are
to flow the purposes of our lives.—*William J. Bryan*

THE TWO ROSES

I HOLD in my hand a rose. Its texture is delicate; its color, beautiful. Every petal is complete and nearly perfect. Everybody loves the beauty and fragrance of the perfect rose. I hold here another. Some of its petals are well developed; others, withered and shriveled. These strikingly resemble two types of people. The rose that has all of its petals well developed is like those people who are honest, truthful, faithful, kind, loving. Everybody loves those of that type of character. This rose with the withered and shriveled petals is like the person whose character is made defective by occasional falsehoods, cheating, unkindness to parents or others. Such characters can never win admiration and love.   *—Popular Educator*

Sing: "Smile Whenever You Can," from *Merry Melodies.*

Birthdays: James Otis, the pen-name of James Otis Kaler, an American writer for young folks, born at Winterport, Me., March 19, 1848; lives in Portland, Me.

William Jennings Bryan, an American statesman and politician, born at Salem, Ill., March 19, 1860; at present (1914) Secretary of State, Washington, D. C.

20 SPRING

Everywhere about us they are glowing,
Some like stars, to tell us Spring is born.
—From "Flowers," by Henry W. Longfellow

Read: "A Laughing Chorus" and "Wild Geese," from *Language Through Nature, Literature and Art.*

Sing: "Spring is Coming," from *Uncle Sam's School Songs.*

Birthdays: Henrik Ibsen, a noted Norwegian poet and writer of plays, born at Skien, Norway, March 20, 1828; died in Christiana, Norway, May 22, 1906.

Charles W. Eliot, an American educator, ex-president of

Harvard University, born in Boston, Mass., March 20, 1834; lives in Cambridge, Mass.

Enrico Caruso, an Italian tenor singer, born in Naples, Italy, March 20, 1874. He sings in more than forty operas.

21   ORANGE DAY

March is merry, March is mad,
March is gay, March is sad;
Every humor we may know
If we list the winds that blow.
—*Frank Dempster Sherman*

CALIFORNIA'S ORANGE DAY

THE great State of California—the Golden State—has set aside one day which is called "Orange Day" (the first day of spring), and to-day is that day.

We ought all to celebrate this day, for the orange, the plum (prune when it is dried), the apple, the peach, the grape—those are nature's most beautiful and precious gifts to man. The orange, provided in the winter months, when peaches, apples and other fruits are hard to get, or entirely lacking, has a value that is not generally understood. It is not only a fruit beautiful and delicious, but one most important to the human race.

Those who admire the apple say, "An apple a day will keep the doctor away." And there is much truth in the statement. It is equally true, in the winter months and all through the hot weather as well, of the orange, a friend of children, a blessing to the human race.

Special Day: First day of spring. California's "Orange Day."

22   SPRING

Would you think it? Spring has come,
Winter's paid his passage home;
Packed his ice-box—gone—half way
To the arctic pole, they say.
—*Christopher Cranch*

Read: "Spring," from *Boston Collection of Kindergarten Stories;* "Spring and Her Helpers," from Poulsson's *In the Child's World.*

Sing: "Wake Up" and "In the Springtime," from *Songs in Season.*

Birthdays: Sir Anthony Van Dyke or Van Dyck, a famous Flemish painter, born in Antwerp, Belgium, March 22, 1599; died in London, England, December 9, 1641.

Johann W. von Goethe, a famous German novel-writer and poet, born in Frankfort-on-the-Main, Germany, August 28, 1749; died in Weimar, Germany, March 22, 1832.

Rosa Bonheur, a famous French painter of animals, born at Bordeaux, France, March 22, 1822; died in Paris, France, May 26, 1899.

23 ANGER

A cheerful temper, joined with innocence, will make beauty attractive, knowledge delightful, and wit good-natured.—*Addison*

THE TWO GARDENERS

Two gardeners had their crops of peas killed by the frost. One of them was very impatient under the loss, and fretted about it. The other patiently went to work to plant a new crop. After awhile the impatient man came to visit his neighbor. To his surprise he found another crop of peas growing finely. He asked how this could be.

"This crop I sowed while you were fretting," said his neighbor.

"But don't you ever fret?" he asked.

"Yes, I do; but I put it off till I have repaired the mischief that has been done."

"Why, then, you have no need to fret at all."

"True," said his friend; "and that's the reason why I put it off."

Read: "Fairy in the Mirror," from *Boston Collection of Kindergarten Stories.*

Birthday: Pierre G. T. Beauregard, an American general, born near New Orleans, La., May 23, 1818; died in New Orleans, February 20, 1893.

24 AIM

Aim well!
No time is lost by care,
Haste fails. Beware! Beware!
A true aim wins, then dare
Make each aim tell.
—*Ella Wheeler Wilcox*

Birthday: William Morris, an English poet and artist, born near London, England, March 24, 1834; died October 3, 1896.

25 EASTER

Sing, children, sing!
And the lily censers swing;
Sing that life and joy are waking and that Death
no more is king.
Sing the happy, happy tumult of the slowly
brightening Spring;
Sing, little children, sing!
—*Celia Thaxter*

EASTER SUNDAY

This Sunday is the festival of our Lord's resurrection, and is one of the most joyous days observed by the Christian church. Coming after the self-denials of Lent and at the beginning of spring, it seems naturally a time of hope and new life. It is the feast of flowers, particularly of lilies, and the name had its origin in a festival in honor of *Eostre,* a Saxon goddess, whose festival was celebrated annually in the spring.

Read: "A Song of Easter," by Celia Thaxter; "The

General's Easter Box," from *Our Holidays: Retold from St. Nicholas;* "First-day Thoughts," by Whittier.

Sing: "Easter," from *Songs in Season.*

Special Day: Easter Day. Easter is the Sunday that follows the 14th day of the calendar moon, which falls upon or next after the 21st of March.

26 NEATNESS

Neatness and its reverse are almost a certain test of moral character.—*Dr. Whitaker*

A NEAT FAMILY

BY LIZZIE DE ARMOND

Tap, tap, young Mr. Woodpecker
Was busy as a bee,
For he had started out to build
Up in the cherry tree.

He cut a dainty little hole,
The chips flew thick and fast,
The entry and the living room
Were finished up at last.

Upon the polished floor was laid
Some shaving mats quite fine,
Where Mrs. Downy Woodpecker
Might ask her guests to dine.

No litter lay around the door
For neighbor folks to see,
Woodpecker said that tidy ways
Ran in his family.

Birthday: Cecil John Rhodes, a South African states-man, born at Bishop Strotford, Hertfordshire, England,

July 5, 1853; died in Cape Town, Africa, March 26, 1902. (Mr. Rhodes made a large fortune in the diamond mine at Kimberley, and left a large part of his money to establish the Rhodes Scholarship.)

27   EXPERIENCE

O, it's I that am the captain of a tidy little ship,
  Of a ship that goes a-sailing on the pond;
And my ship it keeps a-turning all around and all about,
But when I'm a little older, I shall find the secret out,
  How to send my vessel sailing on beyond.
                              —Robert Louis Stevenson

Sing: "What Does Little Birdie Say," from *Merry Melodies.*

Birthday: Oliver Optic, the pen-name of William Taylor Adams, an American writer of books for young folks, born in Medway, Mass., July 30, 1822; died in Boston, Mass., March 27, 1897.

28   ECONOMY

"Waste not, want not," be your motto,
Little things bring weal or woe;
Save the odds and ends, my children,
Some one wants them, if not you.
                              —Mrs. E. R. Miller

WASTE NOT, WANT NOT

A CLERGYMAN called on a wealthy merchant of his congregation, to request a contribution for the church. The merchant made out a check for a large amount.

While sitting at his desk the merchant reproved one of his clerks for throwing away a blank sheet of paper. The clergyman was greatly surprised, for the man had certainly been very generous to the church. Seeing the wondering look, the merchant said:

"If I had not been careful of the little savings I could not now have given you that check."

Sing: "You Never Miss the Water," from *Uncle Sam's School Songs.*

29 INDUSTRY

If little labor, little are our gains;
Man's fortunes are according to his pains.
—*Herrick*

AMY STEWART

THERE was once a little girl named Amy Stewart, who liked to play all day among the flowers and birds. She said they talked to her.

One day her mother said, "You are old enough now, Amy, to do a little work, and you must begin early to be industrious."

"Oh mamma! I do not like to work," said Amy; may I not go in the woods and play before I begin work?"

"As I have nothing ready for you to do just now, you may go for a little while," said her mother.

So Amy ran out of doors. A pretty gray squirrel ran across her path, and she called to him, saying: "Dear squirrel, have you nothing to do but play and eat nuts, have you?"

"Yes," said Mr. Squirrel, "I have a large family to support, and I am busy laying up nuts for the winter, so I cannot stop to play with you."

Just then a bee came buzzing by. Amy said: "Little bee, do you have any work to do?"

"It seems to me I have no time for anything but work, getting honey and making the honeycomb."

Amy now saw an ant carrying off a crumb of bread. "Is not that crumb too heavy for you?" she said. "I wish you would drop it and play with me."

"It is heavy, but I am too glad to get it not to be willing to carry it; but I will stop long enough to tell you of a lazy day we once had. Our home was destroyed, and I was too lazy to help rebuild it; and I said to my brother, 'Let us go and travel; perhaps we will find a house ready-made; perhaps the butterflies will play with us.' We traveled a long way, but we found no ready-made house, and at last were obliged to build one for ourselves. Since then we have been contented to do all the work that we find necessary.''

The ant then picked up the crumb of bread and hurried away.

Amy sat down on a stone and thought: "It seems to me all creatures have some work to do, and they seem to like it; but I do not believe flowers have anything to do. So she walked up to a red poppy and said: "Beautiful red poppy, do flowers work?''

"Of course we do,'' said the poppy. "I have to take great care to gather all the red rays the good sun sends down to me, and I must keep them in my silken petals for you to use, and the green rays must be untangled and held by my glossy leaves, and my roots must drink water, my flowers must watch the days not to let the seed-time pass by—ah, my child, I assure you we are a busy family and that is why we are so happy.''

Amy walked slowly homeward and said to her mother: "The squirrels, the bees, the ants, and even the flowers have something to do. I am the only idle one. Please give me some work to do.''

Then her mother brought her a towel to hem, which she had begun so long before that she had quite forgotten it. She worked very faithfully and in time grew to be an industrious woman, and always said that work made her happier than idleness.

Birthday: John Tyler, tenth president of the United States, born in Greenway, Va., March 29, 1790; died at Richmond, Va., January 17, 1862.

30 KINDNESS

Little acts of kindness,
Little deeds of love,
Make this earth an Eden,
Like the Heaven above.

THE HAPPY-FACED BOY

THIS is what I saw, sitting behind a blackberry bush one lovely spring day, quite out of sight, you understand:

Over the fence jumped a boy, a sweet, happy-faced boy of ten. I knew that he had come from the schoolhouse down the road and was going to the spring which bubbled up under a rock in my meadow. He was eating his luncheon as he walked, had just put the last bit of bread into his mouth, and was looking rather eagerly, as though he enjoyed the prospect very much, at a slice of delicious-looking cake which he held in his hand. Just as he had opened his mouth to take the first bite, his eye fell upon a little pail under a tree not far from my blackberry bush. I had been looking at the little pail, so I knew just what he saw; two slices of bread, that is all, and judging from the appearance of the owner of the pail—who had left it to go to the schoolhouse—that is all there ever was in it. Well, my boy looked at the bread and then at the cake in his hand.

"He shall have half," I heard him say; and he took hold of the cake as though to break it, then paused.

"Half is only a mouthful; he shall have it all;" then, stooping he laid the delicious cake gently in the little pail, and, whistling softly, went on his way to the bubbling spring.

"Ah! no wonder that you are happy-faced, you noble, generous boy!" I said, as I wiped away the tears behind the friendly shelter of the blackberry bush.—*Little Pilgrim*

Birthday: John Fiske, an American historical writer, born in Hartford, Conn., March 30, 1842; died July 4, 1901.

31 FAME

Fame is what you have taken,
Character's what you give;
When to this truth you awaken,
Then you begin to live.
—*Bayard Taylor*

Birthdays: Joseph Haydn, a famous German writer of music, born at Rohran, Lower Austria, March 31, 1732; died in Vienna, Austria, May 31, 1809.

Andrew Lang, a Scottish writer of poems, stories, novels, etc., born at Selkirk, Scotland, March 31, 1844.

APRIL

1 ALL FOOLS' DAY

Good-morning, sweet April,
  So winsome and shy,
With a smile on your lip
  And a tear in your eye;
There are pretty hepaticas
  Hid in your hair,
And bonny blue violets
  Clustering there.

ALL FOOLS' DAY

ALL FOOLS' DAY is so generally observed that a history of its origin will appeal to the interest of pupils.

The day was first celebrated in 1466 at the Court of Burgundy, a province of France. Duke Philip of Burgundy and his court jester, or fool, agreed that on the first day of April each should try his wits to see if he could get the better jest on the other. The terms were that if the jester succeeded in hoaxing the Duke he was to be rewarded with his cap full of gold ducats. If the Duke hoaxed the jester the latter was to forfeit his life. Early in the morning the Duke gave his jester strong drink and the latter partook freely until he became drunk. While he was in this condition the Duke summoned some of the members of the court, tried the drunken jester, and sentenced him to death. The executioner was called, the jester was blindfolded and was struck a mild blow on the neck with a stick under the pretense that it was a sword. Warm blood was then poured on his neck to make him think he was bleeding. The Duke and others standing by laughed heartily at the deception. But the jester lay seemingly lifeless. After a little time some one cried out, "Terror has killed him."

The Duke becoming alarmed sent quickly for the court doctors, who came and tried their skill on the supposed dead man. Soon thereafter the jester opened his eyes, laughed aloud, and said: "April' fools, all of you. Now, Duke, pay me my gold." From this incident of four and a half centuries ago has come the universal custom of jesting on April the first.—*Popular Educator*

Sing: "April! April! Are You Here," from *Songs in Season*.

Birthdays: Prince Otto E. L. Bismarck-Schönhausen, a famous German statesman and one of the greatest men of the nineteenth century, born at Schönhausen, near Magdeburg, Germany, April 1, 1815; died on his estate at Friedrichsruhe, Germany, July 30, 1898.

Edwin Austin Abbey, an American painter, born in Philadelphia, Pa., April 1, 1852; died in London, England, Aug. 1, 1911. Most important work: A series of panels in the Boston Public Library, "The Quest of the Holy Grail."

Special Day: All Fools' Day.

2 FREEDOM

We hold these truths to be self-evident; that all men are created equal; that they are endowed by their Creator with certain inalienable rights; and that among these are life, liberty, and the pursuit of happiness.
—*Jefferson*

HANS CHRISTIAN ANDERSEN

THERE are few children who have not heard of Hans Christian Andersen or who have not read some of his stories. Hans' father, a poor shoemaker, died when Hans was nine years old, and his mother wanted Hans to be a tailor, but he had higher notions. He was first put to work in a factory and then sent to school, but he ran away from both because the boys laughed at his ugliness and awkwardness, and thinking it best to let him do as he pleased, his mother gave him some money to go to Copenhagen. There he was for some time employed in the theater, and for a while lived on charity, but at last became acquainted with the Councillor Collin, who noticing his brightness, got the King to have him educated at the expense of the state. At this time he had written a few poems, and when about finishing his studies he published a book called *A Journey on Foot to Amak*, in which he made fun of everything, and which had a large sale and brought him considerable money. Later he wrote his *Fairy Tales* and *Wonder Stories*. He never walked the streets of Copenhagen without attracting crowds of children. The boys took off their hats to him and the girls courtesied as he passed, and he had a kind word for all. Everybody mourned when he died; and when subscriptions were being taken up to erect a monument to him, all the people were anxious to give something to help honor the poor shoemaker's son who had done so much for the children of all the world.

Read: Andersen's "Five Peas in a Pod" and "The Ugly Duckling."

Birthdays: Thomas Jefferson, third president of the United States, born at Shadwell, Albemarle County, Va., April 2, 1743; died at his estate of Monticello, near Charlottesville, Va., July 4, 1826.

Hans Christian Andersen, a famous Danish writer for young folks, born at Odense, in the island of Fünen, April 2, 1805; died in Copenhagen, Denmark, August 4, 1875.

Frederic A. Bartholdi, a noted French sculptor, born at Colmar, Alsace, France, April 2, 1834; died in Paris, France, October 4, 1904. Among his works are the statues of *Lafayette* in Union Square, New York City, and *Liberty Enlightening the World*, New York Harbor.

Special Day: Arbor Day in Kentucky and Maryland (usually early in April). (See *Arbor Day*, April 19 and 20, this book.)

3 GREATNESS

Little minds are tamed and subdued by misfortune,
but great minds rise above it.—*Washington Irving*

Read: Hale's *The Man Without a Country;* Selections from Irving's *The Sketch Book.*

Sing: "Do Your Best," and "My Country," from Hanson's *Gems of Song.*

Birthdays: Bartolme Esteban Murillo, a famous Spanish painter, born in Seville, Spain, in 1617; died in Seville, April 3, 1682.

Washington Irving, a famous American author, born in New York City, April 3, 1783; died at Sunnyside, his beautiful home at Tarrytown, N. Y., November 28, 1859.

Edward Everett Hale, an American author and clergyman, born in Boston, Mass., April 3, 1822; died in Roxbury, Mass., June 10, 1909.

John Burroughs, an American writer of essays, born at Roxbury, N. Y., April 3, 1837.

4 HELPFULNESS

Look up and not down; look forward and not back;
look out and not in; lend a hand.—*E. E. Hale*

Special Day: Arbor Day in Missouri (Friday after first Tuesday in April). (See *Arbor Day*, April 19 and 20, this book.)

5 KIND WORDS

A soft answer turneth away wrath; but grievous
words stir up anger.—*Solomon*

MORE PRECIOUS THAN RUBIES

WOULD it not please you to pick up strings of pearls, drops of gold, diamonds, and precious stones, as you pass along the street? It would make you feel happy for a month to come. Such a happiness you can give to others. Do you ask how? By dropping sweet words, kind remarks, and pleasant smiles, as you pass along. These are true pearls and precious stones, which can never be lost; of which none can deprive you. Speak to that orphan child; see the diamonds drop from her cheeks. Take the hand of the friendless boy; bright pearls flash in his eyes. Smile on the sad and dejected; a joy suffuses his cheek more brilliant than the most precious stones. By the wayside, amid the city's din, and at the fireside of the poor, drop words and smiles to cheer and bless. You will feel happier when resting upon your pillow at the close of the day, than if you had picked up a score of perishing jewels. The latter fade and crumble in time; the former grow brighter with age, and produce happy reflections forever.—*Selected*

Sing: "Kind Words," from *Uncle Sam's School Songs.*
Birthdays: Jules Dupre, a noted French landscape painter, born at Nantes, France, April 5, 1811; died at L'Isle Adam, France, October 6, 1889.
Algernon Charles Swinburne, an English poet, born in London, England, April 5, 1837; died at Putney, England, April 10, 1909.

6 THE VOICE OF APRIL

April calling, April calling, April calling me!
I hear the voice of April there in each old apple-tree;
Bee-boom and wild perfume, and wood-brook melody,
O hark, my heart, and hear, my heart, the April ecstasy.
—*Madison Cawein*

Read: "The Story of a Seed," from *Language Through Nature, Literature and Art.*

Sing: "Growing," from *Songs in Season.*

Birthday: Raphael (or Raffaelle Sanzio) the greatest of Italian painters, born at Urbino, Italy, April 6, 1483; died April 6, 1520.

7 KNOWLEDGE

> Books are yours,
> Within whose silent chambers treasure lies
> Preserved from age to age; more precious far
> Than that accumulated store of gold
> And orient gems which, for a day of need,
> The sultan hides deep in ancestral tombs.
> These hoards of truth you can unlock at will.
> —*Wordsworth*

SUCCESS IN LIFE

WHEN Dr. Lyman Beecher was asked how long it took him to prepare one of his masterly discourses that had just electrified thousands, he promptly replied, "Forty years."

Birthday: William Wordsworth, a famous English poet, born at Cockemouth, Cumberlandshire, England, April 7, 1770; died at Rydal Mount, England, April 23, 1850.

8 AMBITION

> Better to strive and climb,
>   And never reach the goal,
> Than to drift along with time,
>   An aimless, worthless soul.
> Aye, better climb and fall,
>   Or sow, though the yield be small,
> Than to throw away day after day,
>   And never strive at all.
> —*Margaret Sangster*

Read: "Gonard and the Pine Tree," from Bailey and Lewis' *For the Children's Hour.*

Sing: "Let's Higher Climb," from *Uncle Sam's School Songs.*

9 FLATTERY

No flattery, boy! an honest man can't live by it.
It is a little sneaking art, which knaves
Use to cajole and soften fools withal.
If thou hast flattery in thy nature, out with it,
Or send it to a court where it will thrive.

—Otway

AX GRINDING

BY BENJAMIN FRANKLIN

WHEN I was a little boy, I remember, one cold winter's morning, I was accosted by a smiling man with an ax on his shoulder. "My pretty boy," said he, "has your father a grindstone?"

"Yes, sir," said I.

"You are a fine little fellow!" said he. "Will you let me grind my ax on it?"

Pleased with the compliment of "fine little fellow," "Oh, yes, sir," I answered. "It is down in the shop."

"And will you, my man," said he, patting me on the head, "get me a little hot water?"

How could I refuse? I ran, and soon brought a kettleful.

"How old are you?—and what's your name?" continued he, without waiting for a reply. "I'm sure you are one of the finest lads that I have ever seen. Will you just turn a few minutes for me?"

Tickled with the flattery, like a little fool, I went to work, and bitterly did I rue the day. It was a new ax, and I toiled and tugged till I was almost tired to death. The school bell rang, and I could not get away. My hands were blistered, and the ax was not half ground.

At length, however, it was sharpened, and the man turned to me with, "Now, you little rascal, you've played truant! Scud to the school, or you'll rue it!"

"Alas!" thought I, "it was hard enough to turn a grindstone this cold day, but now to be called a little rascal is too much."

It sank deep into my mind, and often have I thought of it since. When I see a merchant over-polite to his customers, begging them to take a little brandy, and throwing his goods on the counter, thinks I, "That man has an ax to grind."

When I see a man flattering the people, making great professions of attachment to liberty, who is in private life a tyrant, methinks, "Look out, good people! That fellow would set you turning grindstones!"

When I see a man hoisted into office by party spirit, without a single qualification to render him either respectable or useful, "Alas!" methinks, "deluded people, you are doomed for a season to turn the grindstone for a booby."

Birthday: Maria Susanna Cummins, an American novelist, born at Salem, Mass., April 9, 1827; died at Dorchester, Mass., October 1, 1866. Author of *The Lamplighter.*

10 AN APRIL MORNING

A gush of bird song, a patter of dew,
A cloud and a rainbow's warning;
Sudden sunshine and perfect blue—
An April day in the morning.
—*Harriet Spofford*

Birthday: Lewis Wallace, an American soldier and writer, born at Brookville, Ind., April 10, 1827; died February 15, 1905. Best known for his story called *Ben-Hur: A Tale of the Christ.*

11 PERSEVERANCE

Not enjoyment and not sorrow
Is our destined end or way;
But to act that each to-morrow
Find us farther than to-day.
—*From "The Psalm of Life," by Longfellow*

KEEPING AT IT

THERE had been a heavy fall of snow, and a little boy was shoveling a path in front of his mother's door. "How do you expect to get through that deep snow with so small a shovel?" asked a man, who saw that the child was using a coal-shovel.

There was a determined look on the boy's face. "By keeping at it, sir," said the little fellow; "that's how."

"I believe you are right," said the man; "that's the way to do almost anything."

Read: "A Cow His Capital," from Marden's *Stories from Life;* Bible, Prov. 30: 24-28.

Sing: "Time is Short," from *Silvery Notes.*

Birthday: William Ordway Partridge, an American sculptor, born in Paris, France, April 11, 1861; his studio is in New York City.

12 SUCCESS

I would rather be right than president.
—*Henry Clay*

"PRACTICE MAKES PERFECT"

HENRY CLAY, when giving advice to young men, said, "I owe my success in life to one circumstance, that at the age of twenty-seven I began and continued for years, the process of daily reading and speaking upon the contents of some historical or scientific book. These off-hand efforts were made, sometimes in a cornfield, at others in the forest, and not unfrequently in some distant barn, with the horse and the ox for my auditors. It is to this early practice of the art of all arts that I am indebted for the primary and leading impulses that stimulated me onward and have shaped and moulded my whole subsequent destiny."

Birthday: Henry Clay, an American statesman, born near Richmond, Va., April 12, 1777; died June 29, 1852.

13   FAITH

Shall we grow weary in our watch,
  And murmur at the long delay?
Impatient of our Father's time
  And his appointed way?
                              —*Whittier*

UNDER THE LEAVES

BY ALBERT LAIGHTON

OFT have I walked these woodland paths,
  Without the blessed foreknowing
That underneath the withered leaves
  The fairest buds were growing.

To-day the south wind sweeps away
  The types of autumn's splendor,
And shows the sweet arbutus flowers,—
  Spring's children, pure and tender.

O prophet-flowers!—with lips of bloom,
  Outvying in your beauty,
The pearly tints of ocean shells,—
  Ye teach me faith and duty!

Walk life's dark ways, ye seem to say,
  With love's divine foreknowing,
That where man sees but withered leaves,
  God sees sweet flowers growing.

Read: "The King's Birthday," from Lindsay's *Mother Stories.*
Sing: "God's Care," from *Silvery Notes.*

14   TIME

There are no fragments so precious as those of time,
and none so heedlessly lost by people who cannot make
a moment, and yet can waste years.—*Montgomery*

Read: "The Discontented Pendulum" and "What the Clock Told Polly," from Poulsson's *In the Child's World*.

Birthdays: Christian Huygens, a famous Dutch astronomer, born at The Hague, Netherlands, April 14, 1629; died at The Hague, July 8, 1695. Known chiefly for his discoveries in astronomy; is also the inventor of the pendulum clock; and the first watch with a hair-spring was made under his direction and sent to England.

Elbridge S. Brooks, an American writer for young folks, born in Lowell, Mass., April 14, 1846; died January 7, 1902.

15 KINDNESS

How many deeds of kindness
  A little child may do,
Although it has so little strength,
  And little wisdom too!
It wants a loving spirit,
  Much more than strength, to prove
How many things a child may do
  For others, by its love.
                        —*Lucy Larcom*

QUESTIONS

Can you put the spider's web back in its place, that once
    has been swept away?

Can you put the apple again on the bough, which fell at our
    feet to-day?

Can you put the lily-cup back on the stem, and cause it to
    live and grow?

Can you mend the butterfly's broken wing, that you crushed
    with a hasty blow?

Can you put the bloom again on the grape, or the grape
    again on the vine?

Can you put the dewdrop back on the flower, and make
    them sparkle and shine?

Can you put the petals back on the rose? If you could,
    would it smell as sweet?

Can you put the flower again in the husk, and show me the
ripened wheat?
Can you put the kernel back in the nut, or the broken egg
in its shell?
Can you put the honey back in the comb, and cover with
wax each cell?
Can you put the perfume back in the vase, when once it
has sped away?
Can you put the corn-silk back on the corn, or the down
on the catkins—say?
You think my questions are trifling, dear? Let me ask you
another one:
Can a hasty word ever be unsaid, or a deed unkind, undone?
—*Selected*

Birthday: Lucy Larcom, an American writer, born in
Beverly, Mass., 1826; died in Beverly, Mass., April 15, 1893.
Special Days: Arbor Day in Utah. Arbor Day in Ohio
(second or third Friday in April). (See *Arbor Day,* April
19 and 20.)

16 COURTESY

In all the affairs of human life, social as well as
political, I have remarked that courtesies of a small
and trivial character are the ones which strike deepest
to the grateful and appreciating heart.—*Henry Clay*

LINCOLN'S SENTIMENT AND AUTOGRAPH

ABRAHAM LINCOLN once received a letter asking for a
"sentiment" and his autograph. He replied: "Dear
Madam: When you ask from a stranger that which is of
interest only to yourself, always inclose a stamp; there's
your sentiment, and here's your autograph. A. Lincoln."

Tell about the Wright brothers and their invention of the
aeroplane (machine heavier than air, driven by an engine).

Read: "Darius Green and His Flying Machine."
Birthday: Wilbur Wright, an American aeronaut, born near Millville, Ind., April 16, 1867. His brother, also an aeronaut, was born at Dayton, Ohio, Aug. 19, 1871.

17 DAY AND NIGHT

This is the east, where the sun gets up,
  And now we call it day.
He doesn't stop to yawn or fret;
  He has no time to play.

This is the west, where the sun goes to bed;
  Slowly he sinks out of sight,
Then one by one the pretty stars come,
  And now we call it night.
—Miss S. C. Peabody

Sing: "Evening Prayer," from Kellogg's *Best Primary Songs.*

18 WORK

Never you mind the crowd, lad,
  Nor fancy your life won't tell;
The work is done for all that,
  To him who doeth it well.

Fancy the world a hill, lad,
  Look where the millions stop,
You'll find the crowd at the base, lad,
  But there's always room at the top.

Read: "The Boy Who Wanted to Learn," from Cabot's *Ethics for Children* (adapted from Chapter II of *Up from Slavery*, by Booker T. Washington).
Birthdays: Booker Taliaferro Washington, an American writer and educator, born a slave at Hale's Ford, Va., April 18, 1858; lives at Tuskegee, Ala.
Richard Harding Davis, an American author, born in Philadelphia, Pa., April 18, 1864; lives at Mt. Kisco, N. Y.

19 ARBOR DAY

[The Festival of the Trees]

Showers and sunshine bring,
Slowly, the deepening verdure o'er the earth;
To put their foliage out, the woods are slack,
And one by one the singing birds come back.

—Bryant

ARBOR DAY

ARBOR DAY is a designated day upon which the people
and especially the school children plant trees and shrubs
along the highways and other suitable places. It was first
observed in Nebraska. The state board of agriculture
offered prizes for the counties and persons planting the
largest number of trees, and it is said that more than a
million trees were planted the first year, while within six-
teen years over 350,000,000 trees and vines were planted
in the state.

This custom, so beautiful and useful, spread rapidly, and
now is recognized by the statutes of many of the states.

The exact date naturally varies with the climate.

—Our Holidays

Read: Bryant's "The Planting of the Apple-Tree" and
"A Forest Hymn;" Lucy Larcom's "Plant a Tree." See
also Kellogg's *How to Celebrate Arbor Day* for additional
material and suggestions.

Sing: "Arbor Day," from *Songs in Season;* "Happy
Arbor Day" and "The Day of Planting," from *Uncle
Sam's School Songs.*

Special Day: Arbor and Bird Days in Illinois (usually
the third Friday in April and the third Friday in October).

20 ARBOR DAY

[Continued]

When we plant a tree we are doing what we can to
make our planet a more wholesome and happier dwelling place for those who come after us, if not for ourselves.—*Oliver Wendell Holmes*

PLANTING TREES FOR OTHERS

A VERY poor and aged man, busied in planting and grafting an apple tree, was rudely interrupted by this interrogation: "Why do you plant trees, who cannot hope to eat the fruit of them?" He raised himself up, and leaning upon his spade, replied: "Some one planted trees for me before I was born, and I have eaten the fruit; I now plant for others, that the memorial of my gratitude may exist when I am dead and gone."

Birthday: Daniel C. French, an American sculptor, born at Exeter, N. H., April 20, 1850; has his studio in New York City. Among his works are the "Minute Man of Concord," at Concord, Mass., the colossal statue of "The Republic," Columbian Exposition, Chicago, and others.

21 HEROISM

Heroism is simple, and yet it is rare. Every one who does the best he can is a hero.—*Josh Billings.*

Birthdays: Friedrich Froebel, a German teacher, founder of the kindergarten system, born at Oberweissbach, Germany, April 21, 1782; died at Marienthal, Germany, June 21, 1852.

Henry Wheeler Shaw, an American humorist, best known under his pen-name of "Josh Billings," born at Lanesborough, Mass., April 21, 1818; died in Monterey, Cal., October 14, 1885.

John Charles Van Dyke, an American author, born in New Brunswick, N. J., April 21, 1856; lives in New Brunswick.

22 BIRD DAY

There is a bird I know so well,
It seems as if he must have sung
Beside my crib when I was young;
Before I knew the way to spell

The name of even the smallest bird,
His gentle, joyful song I heard.
—*From "The Song Sparrow," by Henry Van Dyke*

Read: Miller's *True Bird Stories;* Bible, Song of Solomon 2:11-12. Have pupils collect and recite quotations about birds from various authors.

Sing: "Bird Day," "The Bluebird," "Little Blue Jay," "Bob White," "Crow Calculations," "Little Bird with Eager Wing," "Robert of Lincoln," "The Sparrow," "The Clacker," all in *Songs in Season*.

Birthday: James Buchanan, fifteenth president of the United States, born at Stony Batter, Franklin County, Pa., April 22, 1791; died on his farm called Wheatlands, at Lancaster, Pa., June 1, 1868.

23   TRUTH

This above all, to thine own self be true;
And it must follow as the night the day,
Thou canst not then be false to any man.
—*Shakespeare*

Read: Story of Shakespeare's life, from *Baldwin's Reader, Book 8; Jones' Reader, Book 4;* or *Cyr's Reader, Book 5.*

Birthdays: William Shakespeare, the greatest English playwriter and poet, born in Stratford-upon-Avon, Warwickshire, England, in April, 1564; died at Stratford-upon-Avon, April 23, 1616.

Joseph M. W. Turner, a famous English painter, born in London, England, April 23, 1775; died in Chelsea, England, December 19, 1851.

Stephen A. Douglas, an American statesman, born in Brandon, Vt., April 23, 1813; died in Chicago, Ill., June 3, 1861.

Edwin Markham, an American poet, born in Oregon City, Ore., April 23, 1852; lives at West New Brighton, N. Y.

Thomas Nelson Page, an American author, born in Hanover County, Va., April 23, 1853.

24   HONOR

Handsome is as handsome does.—Goldsmith

Read: Goldsmith's *The Deserted Village* and *The Vicar of Wakefield;* biography of Goldsmith, from *Baldwin's Reader, Book 7,* or *Cyr's Reader, Book 5.* Biography of Daniel Defoe in *Graded Literature Reader, Book 5;* Bible, Prov. 27:9-10.

Sing: "Robinson Crusoe," from *Songs Every One Should Know.*

Birthdays: Daniel Defoe, a famous English writer, author of *Robinson Crusoe,* born in London, England, in 1661; died in London, April 24, 1731.

Special Day: Arbor Day in Nebraska and (usually) in New Jersey (third Friday in April). (See *Arbor Day,* April 19 and 20.)

25   SELF-SACRIFICE

Hang me to the yard-arm of your ship, if you will,
but do not ask me to become a traitor to my country.
—*Nathan Coffin*

A REAL HERO

THE British troops were occupying Yorktown, which was besieged by the Revolutionary army. Governor Nelson had his residence at Yorktown, and one would suppose that he would have been anxious to protect it. The Federal troops were bombarding the town, when General Lafayette said to Nelson, "To what particular spot would your Excellency direct that we point the cannon?" "There," promptly replied the noble-minded patriot—"to that house; it is mine and is the best one you can find in the town; there you will be most certain to find Lord Cornwallis and the British headquarters.'' This incident is narrated in Custis' life of Washington, a volume which contains many thrilling anecdotes that show the self-sacrificing spirit of those early heroes who by their toils and sufferings laid the foundation of our national life and glory.

Tell the children something about wireless telegraphy and the graphophone.

Sing: "The Battle Prayer," from *Songs Every One Should Know*.

Birthdays: Constance Cary Harrison (Mrs. Burton Harrison), an American writer of novels and stories, born in Virginia, April 25, 1846; lives in Washington, D. C.

Charles Sumner Tainter, an American inventor, born in Watertown, Mass., April 25, 1854; lives in Washington, D. C. He was the inventor of the graphophone.

Guglielmo Marconi, an Italian inventor, born at Griffone, near Bologna, Italy, April 25, 1874. Inventor of wireless telegraphy.

26 CHARACTER

The fruit, when the blossom is blighted, will fall;
The sin will be searched out, no matter how small;
So what you're ashamed to do, don't do at all.
                                        —*Alice Cary*

Read: Alice Cary's "The Pig and the Hen," "A Lesson of Mercy," "Work," "Don't Give Up," and "Old Maxims;" Bible, Prov. 12: 19-22. (See "The Story of Phœbe Cary," September 4, this book.)

Birthdays: Alice Cary, an American poet, born near Cincinnati, Ohio, April 26, 1820; died in New York City, February 12, 1871.

Martha Finley, the pen-name of Martha Farquharson, an American writer for young folks, born in Chillicothe, Ohio, April 26, 1828; died in Elkton, Md., Jan. 30, 1909.

Charles F. Browne (Artemas Warde), an American

humorist, born at Waterford, Me., April 26, 1834; died in Southampton, England, March 6, 1867.

27 TRYING ●

"I'll try" is a soldier,
"I will" is a king;
Be sure they are near
When the school bells ring.

When school days are over,
And boys are men,
"I'll try" and "I will"
Are good friends then.

TOIL SPELLS SUCCESS

SAMUEL F. B. MORSE was the discoverer of the telegraph. The magnetic principle on which the invention depends had been known since 1774, but Professor Morse was the first to apply that principle for the benefit of men. He began his experiments in 1832, and five years afterward succeeded in obtaining a patent on his invention. Then followed another long delay; and it was not until the last day of the session in 1843 that he procured from Congress an appropriation of $30,000. With that appropriation was constructed, between Baltimore and Washington, the first telegraphic line in the world. Perhaps no other invention has exercised a more beneficent influence on the welfare of the human race.

Read: Owen Wister's short life of Ulysses S. Grant.

Birthdays: Samuel F. B. Morse, the inventor of the electric telegraph, born in Charlestown, Mass., April 27, 1791; died in New York City, April 2, 1872.

Herbert Spencer, a famous English philosopher, born in Derby, England, April 27, 1820; died in Brighton, England, December 8, 1903.

Ulysses Simpson Grant, eighteenth president of the

United States, born at Point Pleasant, Ohio, April 27, 1822; died at Mt. Gregor, N. Y., July 23, 1885.

28 POLITENESS

Good manners cannot be put on at pleasure, like an outside coat, but must belong to us.

"THE POLITEST CLERK"

"ONE time when Ulysses S. Grant was in Chicago," said an army official, "he lounged about Sheridan's headquarters a good deal. His son Fred was, at that time, on Sheridan's staff, but was absent one day; and Grant took his place at Fred's desk, to look after the business. A nervous, fidgety, irritable old fellow came in to inquire for some paper that he had left with Fred. When he stated his case, Grant took up the matter in a sympathetic way, and proceeded, after the manner of an over-anxious clerk, to look the paper up. The document could not be found; and Grant, apologizing, walked with the old gentleman to the door. As I walked down the stairs with the mollified visitor, he turned and asked: 'Who is that old codger? He is the politest clerk I ever saw at military headquarters. I hope that Sheridan will keep him.' I answered quietly, 'That is General Grant.' The fidgety old gentleman, after staring at me for a full minute, said, with considerable fervor, 'I will give you fifty cents, if you will kick me downstairs.' "

—*Chicago Tribune*

Read: "The Monroe Doctrine," declaring that the United States would not interfere in any European war, nor permit any European power to get too much influence on this hemisphere. (During Monroe's first term, Illinois, Mississippi and Maine became states of the Union and Spain gave up her possessions in Florida to the United States. Monroe was one of the best presidents this country has ever had.)

Birthdays: James Monroe, fifth president of the United States, born in Westmoreland County, Va., April 28, 1758; died in New York City, July 4, 1831.

James Grant Wilson, an American author, born in New York City, April 28, 1832; lives in New York City.

29 SOWING

The best and highest thing a man can do in a day is to sow a seed, whether it be in the shape of a word, an act, or an acorn.

ARBOR DAY

O PAINTER of the fruits and flowers,
  We thank thee for thy wise design,
Whereby these human hands of ours
  In Nature's garden work with thine.

Give fools their gold; give knaves their power;
  Let fortune's bubbles rise and fall;
Who sows a field, or trains a flower
  Or plants a tree, is more than all.

Special Days: Arbor Day in Michigan and Massachusetts (last Friday in April). Arbor Day in Connecticut (last Friday in April or first Friday in May). Arbor Day in Minnesota and Vermont (latter part of April or first part of May). (See *Arbor Day*, April 19 and 20, this book.)

30 PLEASURES

Pleasures are like poppies spread,
You seize the flower, its bloom is shed;
Or like a snowflake in the river,
A moment white then lost forever.
—*Burns*

THE PLEASURE OF DOING GOOD

A NEWSBOY took the Sixth Avenue elevated railroad cars at Park Place, New York, at noon on Thanksgiving Day, and sliding into one of the cross seats fell asleep. At Grand Street two young women got on and took seats opposite the lad. His feet were bare and his hat had fallen off. Presently one of the young girls leaned over and placed her muff under the little fellow's dirty cheek. An old gentleman smiled at the act, and, without saying anything, held out a quarter with a nod toward the boy. The girl hesitated for a moment and then reached for it. The next man as silently offered a dime, a woman across the aisle held out some pennies, and before she knew it, the girl, with flaming cheeks, had taken money from every passenger in that end of the car. She quietly slipped the amount into the sleeping lad's pocket, removed her muff gently from under his head without arousing him, and got off at Twenty-third street, including all the passengers in a pretty little inclination of her head that seemed full of thanks.   —*Exchange*

Sing: "Merry Springtime," from *Merry Melodies*.

MAY

1 MAY-DAY

Who shall be queen of the May?
  Not the prettiest one, not the wittiest one!
Nor she with the gown most gay!
  But she that is pleasantest all the day through,
  With the pleasantest things to say and to do,—
Oh, she shall be Queen of the May!

MAY-DAY IN ENGLAND

IN ENGLAND the first day of May was in the olden time the most delightful holiday of all the year. It was the day on which the nation expressed its joy at the return of summer. The wild flowers were in bloom and it was sufficiently warm for out-of-door parties. Early in the morning the merry girls often covered themselves with gowns of green leaves and garlands of flowers. The jolly boys blew their horns and waved the branches of trees which they had gathered in the woods. This is what is called bringing home the May.

In the afternoon the children would all meet on the lawn or village green and dance around the Maypole. They would choose one girl to be queen of the May, and would crown her head with flowers and place a mat of flowers under her feet.

Read: Tennyson's "The May Queen;" "May," by Celia Thaxter.

Sing: "The May Queen" and "May Day," from *Songs in Season;* "May," from *Merry Melodies;* "May-Day Song," from *Uncle Sam's School Songs.*

Birthdays: John Dryden, an English poet, born at Aldwinkle, Northamptonshire, England, August 9, 1631; died May 1, 1700.

Joseph Addison, an English author, born at Milston, Wiltshire, England, May 1, 1672; died June 17, 1719.

Arthur W. (Duke of) Wellington, a famous British general and statesman, born near Dublin, Ireland, May 1, 1769; died near Deal, England, Sept. 14, 1852.

George Innes, an American painter, born in Newburgh, N. Y., May 1, 1825; died in Scotland, Aug. 3, 1894. He was one of the best of American landscape painters.

Jules A. Breton, a French painter, born at Courriéres, France, May 1, 1827.

2 ERRORS

Errors, like straws, upon the surface flow,
He who would search for pearls must dive below.
—*Dryden*

Birthdays: Leonardo da Vinci, a famous Italian painter, born near Florence, Italy, in 1452; died near Amboise, France, May 2, 1519.

William Clyde Fitch, an American author and playwright, born in New York City, May 2, 1865; died in France, Sept. 4, 1909.

3 KINDNESS

I shall pass this way but once. Any good thing therefore that I can do, or any kindness that I can show to any human being, let me do it now. Let me not defer it or neglect it, for I shall not pass this way again.
—*Gilpin*

GENEROUS FORBEARANCE

A man who had done Sir Matthew Hale a great injury came afterward to him for his advice in the settlement of his estate. Sir Matthew gave his advice very frankly to him, but would accept of no fee for it; and thereby showed, both that he could forgive as a Christian, and that he had the spirit of a gentleman, not to take money from one who had wronged him so grievously. When he was asked how he could use a man so kindly who had wronged him so much, his answer was, he thanked God he had learned to forget injuries.

Special Days: Arbor Day in Maine (usually the early part of May). Arbor Day in New York (Friday following first day of May). Arbor Day in North Dakota (first Friday in May). (See *Arbor Day*, April 19 and 20, this book.)

4 AUDUBON'S BIRTHDAY

God sent his singers upon earth
With songs of gladness and of mirth
That they might touch the hearts of men
And bring them back to heaven again.
　　　　　　　—*Longfellow*

A LESSON IN PERSEVERANCE

AUDUBON, the celebrated American ornithologist, relates the following story of how he learned a lesson of perseverance under adversity: "An accident," he says, "which happened to two hundred of my original drawings, nearly put a stop to my researches in ornithology. I shall relate it, merely to show how far enthusiasm—for by no other name can I call my perseverance—may enable the preserver of nature to surmount the most disheartening difficulties. I left the village of Henderson, in Kentucky, situated on the banks of the Ohio, where I resided for several years, to proceed to Philadelphia on business. I looked to my drawings before my departure, placed them carefully in a wooden box, and gave them in charge of a relative, with injunctions to see that no injury should happen to them. My absence was of several months; and when I returned, after having enjoyed the pleasures of home for a few days,

I inquired after my box, and what I was pleased to call my treasure. The box was produced and opened; but, reader, feel for me—a pair of Norway rats had taken possession of the whole, and reared a young family among the gnawed bits of paper, which, but a month previous, represented nearly a thousand inhabitants of air! The burning heat which instantly rushed through my brain was too great to be endured without affecting my whole nervous system. I slept for several nights, and the days passed like days of oblivion—until the animal powers being recalled into action through the strength of my constitution, I took up my gun, my note-book and my pencils, and went forth to the woods as gayly as if nothing had happened. I felt pleased that I might now make better drawings than before; and ere a period not exceeding three years had elapsed, my portfolio was again filled.''

Read: Lucy Larcom's ''The Wounded Curlew;'' ''The Birds of Killingsworth;'' ''How the Robin Got Its Red Breast,'' from Cooke's *Nature Myths and Stories;* ''Antics in the Bird Room,'' from Miller's *True Bird Stories.*

Sing: Songs as given under ''Bird Day,'' April 22, this book.

Birthdays: John James Audubon, a celebrated American writer on birds, born in Louisiana, May 4, 1780; died in New York, January 27, 1851.

Horace Mann, an American educator, born at Franklin, Mass., May 4, 1796; died at Yellow Springs, Ohio, August 2, 1859.

William H. Prescott, a famous American historian, born at Salem, Mass., May 4, 1796; died in Boston, Mass., January 28, 1859.

Thomas H. Huxley, an English writer on natural history, born in Middlesex, England, May 4, 1825; died at Eastbourne, England, June 29, 1895.

5 TIME

Use dispatch. Remember that the world only took six days to create. Ask me for whatever you please, except time; that is the only thing which is beyond my power.—*Napoleon*

Birthday: Napoleon Bonaparte, emperor of France, born in Ajaccio, Corsica, August 15, 1769; died on the island of St. Helena, May 5, 1821.

6 GOOD DEEDS

Every gentle word you say,
One dark spirit drives away;
Every gentle deed you do
One bright spirit brings to you.
    —*Virginia Harrison*

Tell about Peary's North Pole expedition and about radium. (A grain of radium about the size of a pin-head is valued at several thousand dollars.)

Birthdays: Robert E. Peary, an American explorer, born at Cresson, Pa., May 6, 1856.

Pierre Curie, a famous French chemist and physicist, born in Paris, France, May 6, 1859; killed by a street accident, April 19, 1906. He and his wife discovered radium.

Frank Dempster Sherman, an American poet, born at Peekskill, N. Y., May 6, 1860; lives in New York City.

7 DUTY

Be a Man!
Bear thine own burden, never think to thrust
Thy fate upon another.
    —*Robert Browning*

Read: "An Incident of the French Camp," by Robert Browning, from *Cyr's Reader, Book 4;* "The Pied Piper," from *Jones' Reader, Book 4;* biography, from *Baldwin's Reader, Book 8.*

Birthdays: Robert Browning (husband of Elizabeth

Barrett Browning), a celebrated English poet, born at Camberwell, near London, England, May 7, 1812; died December 12, 1889.

Johannes Brahms, a famous German composer of music, born in Hamburg, Germany, May 7, 1833; died in Vienna, Austria, April 3, 1897.

8   CHEERFULNESS

A cheerful temper joined with innocence, will make beauty attractive, knowledge delightful, and wit good-natured. It will lighten sickness, poverty and affliction, convert ignorance to an amiable simplicity, and render deformity itself agreeable.—*Addison*

WHERE THE SHINE CAME FROM

"Well, Grandma," said a little boy, resting his elbows on the old lady's stuffed chair-arm, "what have you been doing here at the window all day by yourself?"

"All I could," answered dear Grandma cheerily; "I have read a little, and prayed a good deal and then looked out at the people. There's one little girl, Arthur, whom I have learned to watch for. She has sunny brown hair, and her eyes have the same sunny look in them, and I wonder every day what makes her look so bright. Ah! here she comes now."

Arthur took his elbows off the stuffed arm, and planted them on the window-sill.

"That girl with the brown dress on?" he cried. "Why, I know that girl. That's Susie Moore, and she has a dreadfully hard time, Grandma."

"Has she?" said Grandma. "Well, Arthur, wouldn't you like to know where she gets all that brightness from, then?"

"I'll ask her," said Arthur, promptly; and he raised the window and called:

"Susie, Susie, come up here a minute; Grandma wants to see you!"

The brown eyes opened wide in surprise, but the little maid turned at once and came in.

"Grandma wants to know, Susie Moore," explained the boy, "what makes you look so bright all the time?"

"Why, I have to," said Susie. "You see, Father has been ill a long while, and Mother is tired out with nursing, and the baby is cross with her teeth, and if I were not bright, who would be?"

"Yes, yes, I see," said dear old Grandma, putting her arms around this little ray of sunshine. "Shine on, little girl; there couldn't be a better reason for shining than because it is dark at home."

Read: "Making the Best of It," and "Pippa Passes," from Bailey and Lewis' *For the Children's Hour;* "The Desert" and "The Walled Garden," from Richards' *The Golden Windows.*

Sing: "The Merry Children," from *Merry Melodies.*

Birthday: Augusta Jane (Evans) Wilson, an American novelist, born in Columbus, Ga., May 8, 1835; died in Mobile, Ala., May 9, 1909.

Special Day: Arbor Day in Montana (second Tuesday in May). (See *Arbor Day,* April 19 and 20, this book.)

9 WORK

Ho, all who labor, all who strive!
  Ye wield a mighty power;
Do with your might, do with your strength,
  Fill every golden hour!
The glorious privilege to do
  Is man's most noble dower.
Oh to your birthright and yourselves,
  To your own souls be true!
A weary, wretched life is theirs
  Who have no work to do.
              —Caroline F. Orne

Birthdays: William Bradford, one of the Pilgrim Fathers and second governor of Plymouth colony, born at Austerfield, Yorkshire, England, in 1588; died at Plymouth, Mass., May 9, 1657.

John Brown, an American abolitionist, born in Torrington, Conn., May 9, 1800; hanged at Charlestown, Va., December 2, 1859.

Adolph Schreyer, a German painter, born at Frankfort-on-the-Main, Germany, May 9, 1828; died at Kronberg, Prussia, July 30, 1899.

James Matthew Barrie, a Scottish novelist, born at Kirriemuir, Scotland, May 9, 1860; lives at Kirriemuir. Author of *The Little Minister*, etc.

10 MOTHER'S DAY

[Second Sunday in May]

MOTHER'S DAY

THE idea of a national Mother's Day originated with Miss Anna Jarvis of Philadelphia, and the second Sunday in May was the chosen day. A white carnation was designated as the flower to be worn in honor of Mother.

On this day acts of kindness are done in the home, letters are written to mothers by children away from home, and sermons preached and services held in honor of the mothers of our land.

Many schoolrooms celebrate Mother's Day with programs of recitations and songs on Friday preceding the Sunday chosen for the observance of the occasion.

SOMEBODY'S MOTHER

WHEN our train reached Clinton, the conductor entered the car, and, taking the bundles of a very old lady, carefully helped her to the platform, and then, giving her his arm, conducted her to the waiting room, and placed her bundles beside her. He then signaled the engineer, and boarded the moving train. Struck by this unusual civility to a poor woman, a gentleman said, "I beg your pardon, Mr. Conductor. Was that old lady your mother?" "No," said the conductor, "but she is *somebody's mother.*"

—Sanford

Read: "My Good-for-Nothing," by Emily Huntington Miller; "A Mother's Secret," by O. W. Holmes; "A Mother's Love," by James Montgomery; "O Mother-My-Love," by Eugene Field; "Mother Love," by W. C. Bryant; "Mother Love," by James Whitcomb Riley; "My Mother," by Jane Taylor; "Just a Little Mother," by Margaret Sangster, "Rock Me to Sleep," by Elizabeth Akers.

Sing: "Mother Day," from *Songs in Season.*

Birthdays: Count de Rochambeau, a French soldier, who was sent to command the French troops in America, where he remained helping Washington until peace was declared (1783), when he returned to France, was born in Vendôme, France, July 1, 1725; died in France, May 10, 1807.

James Bryce, a British diplomatist and statesman, born in Belfast, Ireland, May 10, 1838; living at Hindleap, Sussex, England. Distinguished as an author, his best known work being *The American Commonwealth.*

11 MOTHER'S DAY
[Continued]

THE WHITE CARNATION

BY MARGARET E. SANGSTER

Here's to the white carnation,
　　Sturdy and spicy and sweet,
Wafting a breath of perfume
　　On the stony way of the street;

Bringing a thought of gladness
  Wherever the breezes blow;
Here's to the white carnation,
  Pure as the virgin snow.

This is the flower for Mother,
  Wear it on Mother's Day;
Flower for rain and sunshine,
  Winsome, gallant and gay;
Wear it in mother's honor
  Pinned to the coat's lapel;
Wear it in belt and corsage,
  For her who loved you well.

The mother in lowly cabin,
  The mother in palace hall,
Is ever the best and dearest
  The one we love best of all.
In travail and pain she bore us,
  In laughter and love she nursed,
And who that would shame a mother
  Is of all mankind accursed.

Tired and wan too often,
  Weary and weak at times,
But always full of the courage
  That thrills when the future chimes;
Mother with hands toil-hardened,
  Mother in pearls and lace,
The light of heavenly beauty
  Shines in your tender face.

So here's to the white carnation,
  Wear it on Mother's Day;
Flower that blooms for mother,
  Winsome, gallant and gay.

Flower of a perfect sweetness,
Flower for hut and hall,
Here's to the white carnation
And to Mother—Our Best of All.

Birthday: John Brown, a Scottish physician and author, born at Biggar, Lanarkshire, Scotland, September, 1810; died May 11, 1882. Author of *Rab and His Friends.*
Special Day: Arbor Day in Rhode Island (second Friday in May). (See *Arbor Day,* April 19 and 20, this book.)

12 MERCY

Teach me to feel another's woe,
To hide the fault I see;
That mercy I to others show,
That mercy show to me.
—*Pope*

FLORENCE NIGHTINGALE

FLORENCE NIGHTINGALE early exhibited an intense devotion to the alleviation of suffering, which, in 1844, led her to give attention to the condition of hospitals. She visited and inspected civil and military hospitals all over Europe; and in 1851 went into training as a nurse. In 1854 war was declared with Russia, and the hospitals on the Bosphorus soon were crowded with sick and wounded. In this crisis Miss Nightingale offered to go out and organize a nursing-department at Scutari. Lord Herbert accepted her services, and she departed with thirty-four nurses. She arrived at Constantinople, November 4th, on the eve of Inkermann, in time to receive the wounded into wards already filled with 2,300 patients, and a few months after her arrival she had 10,000 sick men under her care. In 1855, while in the Crimea, she was prostrated with fever, but refused to leave her post, and on her recovery remained at Scutari till Turkey was evacuated by the British, July 28, 1856. At the close of the Crimean War a fund of

$250,000 was subscribed for the purpose of enabling her to form an institution for the training of nurses; this is spent in connection with St. Thomas' (the Nightingale Home) and at King's College Hospital.

Read: The story of the life of Florence Nightingale, by Laura E. Richards; Longfellow's "Santa Filomena," which was written in her praise and honor. Tell also the story of Clara Barton (see *The Red Cross*, October 26, this book), who has been to the American soldier what Florence Nightingale was to his British cousin.

Sing: "The Long Weary Day," from *Songs Every One Should Know;* "Nearer, My God, to Thee," from *American School Songs.*

Birthdays: Florence Nightingale, an English lady noted for her care of the sick and wounded in the Crimean War, born of English parents, in Florence, Italy, May 12, 1820; died in London, England, August 13, 1910.

Henry Cabot Lodge, an American historian, born in Boston, Mass., May 12, 1850.

13 GOODNESS

Ring in new school-books and new toys;
Ring out all things that ruin boys;
Ring out the smoker and the smoke;
Ring out old habit's ugly yoke.
Ring out the swearer from the street;
Ring out the fighter and the cheat;
Ring out the child that doesn't care;
Ring in good children everywhere.

14 GREATNESS

From a little spark may burst a mighty flame.
—*Dante*

15 LITTLE THINGS

Little moments make an hour;
Little thoughts, a book;
Little seeds, a tree or flower;
Water-drops, a brook;
Little deeds of faith and love
Make a home for you above.

16 RIGHT AND WRONG

Little by little the world grows strong,
Fighting the battles of right and wrong;
Little by little the wrong gives way;
Little by little the right has sway;
Little by little all longing souls
Struggle up near the shining goals.

KEEP TO THE RIGHT

"Keep to the right," as the law directs,
For such is the rule of the road:
Keep to the right, whoever expects
Securely to carry life's load.

Keep to the right, with God and his word;
Nor wander, though folly allure;
Keep to the right, nor ever be turned
· From what's faithful and holy and pure.

Keep to the right, within and without,
With stranger and kindred and friend;
Keep to the right, and you need have no doubt,
That all will be well in the end.

Keep to the right in whatever you do,
Nor claim but your own on the way;
Keep to the right, and hold on to the true,
From the morn to the close of life's day.

Read: "The Immortal Fountain," from Poulsson's *In the Child's World;* "The Little Girl with the Light," from Lindsay's *Mother Stories.*

Birthdays: Honoré de Balzac, a noted French writer of novels, born at Tours, France, May 16, 1799; died in Paris, France, August 20, 1850.

William Henry Seward, a noted American statesman,

born in Florida, Orange County, N. Y., May 16, 1801; died in Auburn, N. Y., October 10, 1872.

17   DEEDS

We live in deeds, not years; in thoughts, not breaths;
In feelings, not in figures on a dial.
We should count time by heart-throbs. He most lives
Who thinks most, feels the noblest, acts the best.
—*P. J. Bailey*

A BENEFACTOR OF MANKIND

EDWARD JENNER, a noted English physician, made the discovery that vaccinating people with cow-pox would save them from taking smallpox, a disease long common in Europe. He got his idea from hearing that peasants who had accidentally caught the cow-pox from milking cows diseased with it were free from smallpox. He worked many years to find a sure way of vaccinating one person from another, as well as from the pock of a cow; and although he proved it a success, it took many years more to get the London physicians to believe it. At last, about the year 1800, vaccination began to be widely practiced, and soon spread all over the globe. Wealth and honor were bestowed on Dr. Jenner, and he was called a benefactor of mankind.

Birthday: Edward Jenner, a noted English physician, born in Berkeley, Gloucestershire, England, May 17, 1749; died at Berkeley, January 26, 1823.

18   PEACE DAY

Peace has her victories,
No less renown'd than war.
—*Milton*

THE HAGUE PEACE CONFERENCE

ON THE 18th of May, 1899, the Czar of Russia called the first peace conference at The Hague, in Holland, and one hundred representatives met in that city, in Queen Wilhelmina's little palace called "The Home in the Woods." For three months they sat behind closed doors in a circular hall decorated with large paintings commemorating the Peace of Munster. In that hall is inscribed the motto "The greatest victory is that by which peace is won." The results of that conference were as follows: A permanent international tribunal was established with over seventy permanent judges, four of whom were to be appointed by the United States. That tribunal opened in 1901. Andrew Carnegie donated $1,500,000 for the erection of a building. The first case before that tribunal was submitted by the United States and Mexico. By its provisions for mediation President Roosevelt made possible the Portsmouth treaty between Japan and Russia.

The second Hague conference met June 15, 1907, representatives of all the nations of the globe were present. and it was in session four months. It was the most august assembly in human history. Some of the important matters that failed of the unanimous acceptance necessary were accepted by a large majority. Provision was made for a third conference to assemble within eight years. A world court was agreed upon to try cases by international law. That court has fifteen judges, and in addition to it there is a tribunal of arbitration. Notable harmony and courtesy existed among all the delegates. Several nations, among them the five Central American states, have agreed to arbitrate every question arising between them.

> O! make Thou us through centuries long,
> In peace secure, in justice strong;
> Around our gift of freedom draw
> The safeguard of Thy righteous law.
> —*Whittier*

Read: "Angel of Peace," by O. W. Holmes; "The People's Song of Peace," by Joaquin Miller.

Sing: "The Message of Peace," "The Dawn of Peace,"

and "The Song of Peace," from *May Intermediate Plan Book*, by Marian M. George.

Special Day: Peace Day, the 18th day of May.

19 CHARACTER

> No fountain is so small but that heaven may be imaged in its bosom.—*Hawthorne*

Read: Biography of Hawthorne, from *Jones' Reader, Book 4; The Great Stone Face; The Miraculous Pitcher.*

Birthday: Nathaniel Hawthorne, a famous American author, born in Salem, Mass., July 4, 1804; died in Plymouth, Mass., May 19, 1864.

20 DUTY

> So nigh is grandeur to our dust,
>   So near is God to man,
> When Duty whispers low, *Thou must*,
>   The youth replies, *I can.*
> —*Emerson*

Birthday: Albert Dürer, a noted German painter and engraver, born in Nuremberg, Germany, May 20, 1471; died in Nuremberg, April 6, 1528.

21 FLOWER DAY

> Dear common flower, that grow'st beside the way,
> Fringing the dusty road with harmless gold,
> First pledge of blithesome May.
> —*From "To a Dandelion," by Lowell*

Read: "Little Ida's Flowers" and "Angel" from Andersen's *Wonder Stories;* "Garden Farm," from Richards' *More Five Minute Stories.* Have pupils collect and recite quotations about flowers from various authors.

Sing: "Pansies," "Daisies in the Meadows," "Forget-Me-Not," "A Sweet Pea," "Stars and Posies," "Buttercups and Daisies" and "Daisy Nurses" from *Songs in Season.*

22 ORDER

Order is Heaven's first law.—*Pope*

Birthdays: Alexander Pope, a famous English poet, born in London, England, May 22, 1688; died at Twicken-ham, England, May 30, 1744.

Richard Wagner, a famous German writer of music and poetry, born in Leipsic, Germany, May 22, 1813; died at Venice, Italy, February 13, 1883.

Sir Arthur Conan Doyle, a British novelist, born in Edinburgh, Scotland, May 22, 1859; lives at Hindhead, Surrey, England.

23 DOING GOOD

He liveth long who liveth well;
  All else is life but flung away;
He liveth longest who can tell
  Of true things truly done each day.

Sow love, and taste its fruitage pure;
  Sow peace, and reap its harvest bright;
Sow sunbeams on the rock and moor.
And find a harvest home of light.
                    H. Bonar

24 CLEANLINESS

Cleanliness may be defined to be the emblem of purity of mind.—*Addison*

NEIGHBOR MINE

THERE are barrels in the hallways,
    Neighbor mine,
Pray be mindful of them always,
    Neighbor mine.
If you're not devoid of feeling,
Quickly to those barrels stealing,
Throw in each banana peeling,
    Neighbor mine.

Look! where'er you drop a paper,
　　Neighbor mine,
In the wind it cuts a caper,
　　Neighbor mine.
Down the street it madly courses,
And should fill you with remorses,
When you see it scare the horses,
　　Neighbor mine.

Paper cans were made for papers,
　　Neighbor mine,
Let's not have the fact escape us,
　　Neighbor mine.
And if you will lend a hand,
Soon our city dear shall stand
As the cleanest in the land,
　　Neighbor mine.

Read: Bible, Psalm 24:4.

Birthday: Sir Arthur W. Pinero, an English dramatist, born in London, England, May 24, 1855; lives in London.

25 LIFE IS SHORT ·

Life is too short to waste in critic peep or cynic bark,
Quarrel or reprimand; 'twill soon be dark;
Up! mind thine own aim, and God speed the mark.
　　　　　　　　　　　　　　　—*Emerson*

Read: "Forbearance," "Each and All," "The Mountain and the Squirrel," "Friendship" and "Days," by Emerson.

Birthdays: Ralph Waldo Emerson, a noted American writer, born in Boston, Mass., May 25, 1803; died at Concord, Mass., April 27, 1882.

Edward G. E. Bulwer-Lytton, a famous English writer, born in London, England, May 25, 1803; died at Torquay, Devonshire, England, January 18, 1873.

26 BEAUTY

I know blue modest violets,
Gleaming with dew at morn—
I know the place you came from,
And the way that you were born!
When God cuts holes in heaven,
The holes the stars look through,
He lets the scraps fall down to earth,
The little scraps are you.

—*Phœbe Cary*

27 HONOR

From our ancestors come our names, but from our honesty our honor.

OUR PRESIDENTS IN RHYME

BY JEANNIE PENDLETON EWING

WITH Washington's name did the President's start—
"First in war, first in peace and each countryman's heart."
Then Adams, and then Thomas Jefferson, who
Wrote the great Declaration for me and for you.
Two Jameses—James Madison, and then James Monroe,
And John Quincy Adams came next, you should know.
Next Jackson, Van Buren; when Harrison died
Vice-President Tyler succeeded with pride.
Polk, Taylor, and Fillmore, in turn, and then Pierce,
With Buchanan and Lincoln as war-times loomed fierce.
Johnson, Grant, Hayes and Garfield; when Garfield was
    killed,
His term by Vice-President Arthur was filled.
Cleveland, Harrison; Cleveland again for a term,
Then William McKinley, a good man and firm.
Next, Roosevelt, hunter and President great,
Good soldier in battle, and good, too, in State.
And then Mr. Taft, till the March day and hour
When President Wilson succeeds him in power.

—*Popular Educator*

Birthdays: Nathanael Greene, a noted American general, born at Potowhommet, R. I., May 27, 1742; died near Savannah, Georgia, June 19, 1786.

Julia Ward Howe, an American poet, born in New York, N. Y., May 27, 1819; died in Portsmouth, R. I., Oct. 17, 1910.

John Kendrick Bangs, an American author and editor, born at Yonkers, N. Y., May 27, 1862; lives at Yonkers.

28 MEMORY

Let Fate do her worst; there are relics of joy,
Bright dreams of the past, which she cannot destroy.
They come in the night-time of sorrow and care,
And bring back the features that joy used to wear.
Long, long be my heart with such memories filled,
Like a vase in which roses have once been distilled;
You may break, you may shatter the vase if you will
But the scent of the roses will hang round it still.

—*Moore*

Read: Selections from Moore's poems.

Sing: "The Last Rose of Summer," "The Minstrel Boy" and "The Harp that Once thro' Tara's Halls," from *Songs Every One Should Know*.

Birthdays: Thomas Moore, a famous Irish poet, born in Dublin, Ireland, May 28, 1779; died at Bromham, February 25, 1852.

Louis J. R. Agassiz, a noted teacher of natural history, born in Motiers, Switzerland, May 28, 1807; died in Cambridge, Mass., December 14, 1873.

29 PATRIOTISM

I know not what course others may take, but as for me, give me liberty or give me death!

—*Patrick Henry*

PATRICK HENRY

WHEN Patrick Henry grew to be a man he went into business, but failed twice; he then became a lawyer, but for three years got very little practice, when by some lucky chance he was chosen as lawyer in a case called the "Parsons' Cause" because it was a quarrel between the parsons and the planters. To the surprise of everybody, Henry made a wonderful speech, and though he lost his case, from that time he was famous. He soon became the leader of the people's party, and when a member of the legislature (1765), he took a strong stand against the Stamp Act; and in his speech against it used these celebrated words: "Caesar had his Brutus, Charles I. his Cromwell, and George III." (here people cried out 'Treason!') "may profit by their example. If this be treason, make the most of it." In 1774 he was the first speaker of the General Congress which met in Philadelphia. The next year he made his famous speech in Virginia in favor of putting the colony in a state of defense, in which he concluded: "I know not what course others may take, but as for me, give me liberty or give me death!" Patrick Henry was twice Governor of Virginia, and refused many high offices.

Birthday: Patrick Henry, a famous American orator and statesman, born in Hanover County, Va., May 29, 1736; died at Red Hill, Va., June 16, 1799.

30 MEMORIAL DAY

For the dead, a tribute;
For the living, a memory;
For posterity, an emblem of loyalty to the
    flag of their country.
—*Inscription on Soldiers' Monument, Pittsfield, Mass.*

MEMORIAL DAY

With slow and reverent tread
I bring the roses red,
To deck the soldier's bed,
Emblem of blood they shed
For this our native land.

And I, white daisies bring,
A simple offering;
Emblem of holy peace,
Oh, may its reign ne'er cease
In this our happy land.

I bring the violets blue,
They say, "Be true, be true,
True to the friends that love you,
True to the God above you
And to thy native land."

Read: Lincoln's "Gettysburg Address," "The Blue and the Gray," by Francis M. Finch; "Cover Them Over," by Will Carleton.

Sing: "America," "The Star-Spangled Banner," "Columbia, the Gem of the Ocean," "Battle Hymn of the Republic," "We're Tenting To-night"; also "Memorial Day" and "The Blue and the Gray Together," from *Songs in Season*.

Birthday: Alfred Austin, an English poet and critic, born at Headingly, near Leeds, England, May 30, 1835. He succeeded Tennyson as Poet Laureate, in 1896.

31 MEMORIAL DAY

[Continued]
Furl the banner, softly, slowly,
Treat it gently, it is holy—
For it droops above the dead.
—*Ryan*

Memorize extracts from Daniel Webster's "Bunker Hill Oration."

Birthday: Walt Whitman, an American poet, born at West Hills, Long Island, N. Y., May 31, 1819; died in Camden, N. J., March 26, 1892.

JUNE

1 GREATNESS

Lives of great men all remind us,
    We can make our lives sublime,
And departing, leave behind us
    Footprints in the sands of time.

Footprints, that perhaps another,
    Sailing o'er life's solemn main,
A forlorn and shipwreck'd brother,
    Seeing, shall take heart again.
                      —*Ibid*

2 FORGIVENESS

If those who've wronged us own their faults and kindly pity pray,
When shall we listen and forgive? To-day, my love, to-day.
But if stern justice urge rebuke, and warmth from memory borrow,
When shall we chide, if chide we must? To-morrow, love, to-morrow.

A NOBLE EXAMPLE

JOSEPH BRADFORD was for many years the traveling companion of the Rev. John Wesley, and considered no assistance to him too servile, but was subject to changes of temper. Wesley directed him to carry a package of letters to the post; Bradford wished to hear his sermon first; Wesley was urgent and insisted; Bradford refused. "Then," said Wesley, "you and I must part." "Very good, sir," replied Bradford.

They slept over it. On rising the next morning Wesley accosted his old friend and asked if he had considered what he had said, that "they must part." "Yes, sir," replied Bradford. "And must we part?" inquired Wesley.

"Please yourself, sir," was the reply. "Will you ask my pardon?" rejoined Wesley. "No, sir." "You won't?" "No, sir." "Then I will ask yours!" replied the great man. Bradford melted under the example, and wept like a child.

Read: "A Hero from Valley Forge," from *An American Book of Golden Deeds;* Bible, Matt. 5:7-9.

Sing: "Rock of Ages," from *Uncle Sam's School Songs.*

Birthdays: John Randolph, of Roanoke, an American orator, born in Chesterfield County, Va., June 2, 1773; died in Philadelphia, Pa., June 24, 1833.

John Godfrey Saxe, an American writer, born in Highgate, Vt., June 2, 1816; died at Albany, N. Y., March 31, 1887.

3 GOODNESS

I wish that friends were always true,
And motives always pure;
I wish the good were not so few;
I wish the bad were fewer.
—*J. G. Saxe*

Birthday: Jefferson Davis, an American statesman and president of the Confederate States during the Civil War, born in Christian County, Kentucky, June 3, 1808; died in New Orleans, La., December 6, 1889.

4 KINDNESS

Little deeds of kindness, little words of love,
Make our earth an Eden like the heaven above.
—*Frances S. Osgood*

ABRAHAM LINCOLN AND HIS MOTHER

ABRAHAM LINCOLN was devotedly attached to his step-mother. When he became a man he often spoke of her as his "saintly mother," his "angel of a mother."

She, herself, late in life, could not speak of him without tears, so great was her affection for him.

"Abe," she said, "was kind, and good, and true. He never gave me a cross word, and never refused to do anything I asked him. He was dutiful and obedient to me always, and I think he loved me truly."

5 LOVE

There is beauty in the sunlight,
And the soft blue heaven above;
Oh, the world is full of beauty,
When the heart is full of love.
—*W. S. Smith*

6 PATRIOTISM

I only regret that I have but one life to give for my country.—*Nathan Hale*

CAPTAIN NATHAN HALE

AFTER Washington's famous retreat from Long Island during the Revolutionary War, he wished to learn something about the plans of the English general, Howe. When volunteers were called for to attempt the hazardous undertaking of crossing the enemy's lines for information, brave Capt. Nathan Hale cheerfully offered to go, and Washington intrusted him with the important duty. His mission was completed and just as he was returning a Tory relative discovered the identity of Capt. Hale, causing his arrest as a spy. The next morning, after being treated cruelly by the British and refused the use of his Bible, he was hung as a spy. Letters that he had written to his sisters and mother were destroyed by his unsympathetic captors. He died like a brave man, saying: "I regret that I have but one life to give for my country."

Read: "Nathan Hale," by *Francis Miles Finch.*

Birthdays: Nathan Hale, an American soldier and

patriot, born in Coventry, Conn., June 6, 1755; hanged as
a spy in New York City, September 22, 1776.

John Trumbull, an American painter, born in Lebanon,
Conn., June 6, 1756; died in New York City, November
10, 1843.

7 TRUE DIGNITY

True dignity abides with him alone
Who, in the patient hour of silent thought,
Can still respect and still revere himself.
—*Wordsworth*

ASSOCIATION

THERE are localities in Switzerland where the canary is
caged with the nightingale so that it may catch the sweetness and breathe into its notes that harmonious melody
that delights all tourists in Europe. It is a demonstration
of association.

So men may make their lives strong, pure, sweet and
holy in thought, word, and deed by unbroken association
with those who live on a higher plane.

—*Popular Educator*

Birthday: Richard D. Blackmore, an English novelist,
born at Longworth, Berkshire, England, June 7, 1825;
died January 21, 1900. Author of *Lorna Doone,* etc.

8 DUTY

The boys and girls who do their best,
Their best will better grow;
But those who slight their daily task,
They let the better go.

Birthdays: Charles Reade, a famous English novelist,
born at Ipsden House, Oxfordshire, England, June 8, 1814;
died in London, April 11, 1884. Author of *The Cloister
and the Hearth.*

Sir John Everett Millais, an English painter, born in

Southampton, England, June 8, 1829; died in London, England, August 31, 1896.

9 PERSEVERANCE

In the lexicon of youth, which fate reserves for a bright manhood, there is no such word as fail.
— *Bulwer-Lytton*

"PERSEVERE"

GEORGE STEPHENSON, when addressing young men, was accustomed to sum up his best advice to them in the words: "Do as I have done—persevere." He was the son of a poor colliery laborer, and when fourteen years old became an assistant fireman in the colliery. He had not learned to read until he was eighteen. But when he was placed in charge of an engine he studied it so carefully that he could take it to pieces and put it together again. The engines of those days were stationary, and locomotives were unknown. People had often said what a good thing it would be if some-body only would invent an engine to draw wagons; but the wise shook their heads and said that was impossible. Stephenson soon showed them it was quite possible to make an engine that would go, but he spent fifteen hard years working at the improvement of his locomotive before achieving his decisive victory at Rainhill. This is only one of many striking illustrations showing how by patient trying success has been won in every branch of science, art, and industry.

Sing: "Home, Sweet Home."

Birthdays: George Stephenson, a noted English railway engineer, the inventor of the locomotive, born at Wylam, Northumberland, England, June 9, 1781; died at his estate of Tapton Park, England, August 12, 1848.

John Howard Payne, an American writer and actor, born

in New York, June 9, 1792; died in Tunis, April 10, 1852. Author of the song, "Home, Sweet Home."

Francis Miles Finch, an American lawyer, and poet, born at Ithica, N. Y., June 9, 1827; died in Ithica, July 31, 1907. Author of poems, "Nathan Hale" and "The Blue and the Gray."

10 OBEDIENCE

He who has learned to obey, will know how to command.—*Solon*

Birthdays: Peter I, called Peter the Great, emperor of Russia, fifth of the house of Romanoff, born near Moscow, Russia, June 10, 1672; died in St. Petersburg, February 8, 1725.

Karl Hagenbeck, a German animal trainer and menagerie owner, born in Hamburg, Germany, June 10, 1845.

11 NOBILITY

Beautiful faces are those that wear
The light of a pleasant spirit there;
It matters little if dark or fair.

Beautiful hands are those that do
Deeds that are noble, good, and true;
Busy with them the long day through.

Beautiful feet are those that go
Swiftly to lighten another's woe,
Through the summer's heat or winter's snow.

Beautiful children, if rich or poor,
They walk the pathways sweet and pure
That lead to the mansion strong and sure.

Birthdays: Joseph Warren, a noted American patriot, born in Roxbury, Mass., June 11, 1741. Killed in the battle of Bunker Hill, June 17, 1775.

Mrs. Humphrey Ward, an English novelist, born in Hobart, Tasmania, June 11, 1851. (Her maiden name was

Mary Augusta Arnold, she being a granddaughter of Dr. Thomas Arnold of Rugby, and a niece of Matthew Arnold.)

Richard Strauss, a German composer, born in Munich, Germany, June 11, 1864; lives in Berlin, Germany.

12 HONESTY

Do what conscience says is right;
Do what reason says is best;
Do with all your mind and might;
Do your duty and be blest.

Birthday: Charles Kingsley, a famous English clergyman and writer, born in Holne, Devonshire, England, June 12, 1819; died at Eversley, England, January 23, 1875.

13 RESPECT FOR THE AGED

Be kind and be gentle
To those who are old,
For dearer is kindness,
And better, than gold.

SPARTAN RESPECT FOR THE AGED

THERE was a great play at the principal theater in Athens one night. The seats set apart for strangers were filled with Spartan boys; and other seats, not far distant, were filled with Athenian youth. The theater was crowded, when an old man, infirm, and leaning on a staff, entered. There was no seat for him. The Athenian youth called to the old man to come to them, and with great difficulty he picked his way to their benches; but not a boy rose and offered him a seat. Seeing this, the Spartan boys beckoned to the old man to come to them, and, as he approached their benches, every Spartan boy rose, and, with uncovered head, stood until the old man was seated, and then all quietly resumed their seats. Seeing this, the Athenians broke out in loud applause. The old man rose, and, in a voice that filled the theater, said, "The Athenians know what is right: the Spartans do it."—*White's School Management*

Birthday: Winfield Scott, an American general, born at Petersburg, Va., June 13, 1786; died at West Point, N. Y., May 29, 1866.

14   FLAG DAY

One flag, one land,
One heart, one hand,
One nation evermore.
—*Holmes*

THE SCHOOL-HOUSE STANDS BY THE FLAG

BY HEZEKIAH BUTTERWORTH

Ye who love the Republic, remember the claim
Ye owe to her fortunes, ye owe to her name,
To her years of prosperity past and in store,
A hundred behind you, a thousand before.
    'Tis the school-house that stands by the flag,
        Let the nation stand by the school;
    'Tis the school-bell that rings for our Liberty old,
    'Tis the school-boy whose ballot shall rule.

The blue arch above us is Liberty's dome,
The green fields beneath us, Equality's home.
But the schoolroom to-day is Humanity's friend,—
Let the people the flag and the school-house defend.
    'Tis the school-house that stands by the flag,
        Let the nation stand by the school;
    'Tis the school-bell that rings for our Liberty old,
    'Tis the school-boy whose ballot shall rule.

Read: "The Flag Goes By," by Henry H. Bennett; "An American in Europe," by Henry van Dyke; Whittier's "Barbara Frietchie"; "The Heroine of Fort Henry,"

from Baldwin's *American Book of Golden Deeds;* "The
Stars and Stripes," from *Our Holidays: Retold from St.
Nicholas;* "Betsy Ross; Our Flag," from Wilson's *History
Reader.*

Sing: "The First Flag," "The Salute," and "The Red,
White, and Blue," from *Songs in Season;* "Flag of the
Free," "Columbia, the Gem of the Ocean," and "Flag of
the Stars I Love," from *American School Songs;* "Hurrah
for the Flag!" from Howliston's *Child's Song Book.*

15 FLAG DAY
[Continued]

Red, White and Blue, wave on!
Never may sire or son
   Thy glory mar.
Sacred to liberty,
Honored on land and sea,
Unsoiled forever be,
   Each stripe and star.

WHAT IS A FLAG WORTH?

"HERE'S a ——, but I won't offer that old rag for sale.
Too ragged; clerk, take it away!"

"I'll give five cents for it," shouted a ragman that
chanced to be present. "And I'll give ten dollars for it,"
thundered a man near the door, stepping forward, the
money in his hand.

The auctioneer looked dumbfounded. "It's an American flag," said the man, holding it up before the people.
"Is there a man here that says the AMERICAN FLAG is not
worth ten dollars?"

Learn: "A Salute to the Flag," by Charles Sumner:

"White for purity, red for valor, blue for justice, the
flag of our country, to be cherished by all our hearts, to
be upheld by all our hands."

Birthday: Harriet Elizabeth Beecher Stowe, a noted

American writer, born at Litchfield, Conn., June 15, 1812; died at Hartford, Conn., July 1, 1896.

16   FLAG SALUTE

[Adopted by the National Societies G. A. R. and W. C. R.]

We give our heads and our hearts to God and our country.   One country, one language, one flag.

First Signal: The pupils having been assembled and being seated, and the flag borne by the standard bearer being in front of the school, at the signal (either by a chord struck on the piano or, in the absence of a piano, from a bell) each scholar seizes the seat preparatory to rising.

Second Signal: The whole school rises quickly, as one person, erect and alert.

Third Signal: The right arm is extended. pointing directly at the flag; as the flag bearer should be on the platform where all can see the colors, the extended arm will be slightly raised above a horizontal line.

Fourth Signal: The forearm is bent so as to touch the forehead lightly with the tip of the fingers of the right hand. The motion should be quick, but graceful, the elbow being kept down and not allowed to "stick out" to the right. As the fingers touch the forehead, each pupil will exclaim in a clear voice, "We give our heads" (emphasizing the word "heads").

Fifth Signal: The right hand is carried quickly to the left side and placed flat over the heart, with the words, "and our hearts!" (after the movement has been made).

Sixth Signal: The right hand is allowed to fall quickly, but easily, to the right side; as soon as the motion is accomplished, all will say, "to God and our country!"

Seventh Signal: Each scholar still standing erect, but without moving, will exclaim, "One country!" (emphasis on "country").

Eighth Signal: The scholars, still standing motionless, will exclaim, "One language!" (emphasis on "language").

Ninth Signal: The right arm is suddenly extended to its full length, the hand pointing to the flag, the body inclining slightly forward, supported by the right foot slightly advanced. The attitude should be one of intense earnestness. The pupil reaches, as it were, toward the flag, at the same time exclaiming with great force, "One flag!"

Tenth Signal: The right arm is dropped to the side and the position of attention recovered.

Eleventh Signal: Each scholar seizes the seat preparatory to turning it down.

Twelfth Signal: The school is seated.

Flag Bearer: The color bearer grasps the staff at the lower end with his right hand and a foot or more (according to the length of the staff) above the end of the staff with his left hand. The staff is held directly in front of the middle of the body, slightly inclined forward from the perpendicular. At the fourth signal, the flag will be dipped, returning the salute; this is done by lowering the left hand until the staff is nearly horizontal. keeping it in that position until the tenth signal, when it will be restored to its first, or nearly vertical, position.

Birthday: Wesley Merritt, an American soldier, born in New York City. June 16, 1836; died at Natural Bridge, Va., December 3, 1910.

17 HELPFULNESS

A sense of an earnest will
  To help the lowly living.
And a terrible heart thrill,
  If you have no power of giving;
An aim to aid the weak,
  A friendly hand to the friendless,
Kind words so short to speak,
  But whose echo is endless;

The world is wide, these things are small,
They may be nothing, but they are all.
                                        —*Milnes*

Birthdays: John Wesley, a famous English clergyman, founder of the Methodists, born at Epworth, Lincolnshire, England, June 17, 1703; died in London, March 2, 1791.

Charles Francois Gounod, a noted French writer of music, born in Paris, France, June 17, 1818; died in Paris, October 18, 1893. Wrote the opera *Faust*.

Special Day: Anniversary of the Battle of Bunker Hill (June 17, 1775).

18 BOOKS

Thought is the seed of action.—*Emerson*

THE PARADOX OF BOOKS

BY HANNAH MORE

I'm strange contraditions; I'm new and I'm old,
I'm often in tatters, and often decked with gold.
Though I never could read, yet lettered I'm found;
Though blind, I enlighten; though loose, I am bound.
I'm always in black, and I'm always in white;
I am grave and I'm gay, I am heavy and light.
In form too I differ,—I'm thick and I'm thin;
I've no flesh and no bone, yet I'm covered with skin;
I've more points than the compass, more stops than the flute;
I sing without voices, without speaking confute;
I'm English, I'm German, I'm French, and I'm Dutch;
Some love me too fondly, some slight me too much;
I often die soon, though I sometimes live ages,
And no monarch alive has so many pages.

Birthday: David D. Porter, an American naval commander, born in Philadelphia, Pa., June 18, 1813; died February 13, 1891.

19 EXTRAVAGANCE

Beware of little extravagances; a small leak will
sink a big ship.—*Benjamin Franklin*

FARRAGUT'S RESOLUTION

WHEN Admiral Farragut's son was ten years old the
father said in his hearing that when he was old enough to
make a contract and keep it, he had a bargain to offer him.
The son rose up and asked the father what the contract
was. The Admiral said, "The proposal I intend to make
is this: If you will not smoke or chew tobacco, drink in-
toxicating or strong wines, till you are twenty-one years
of age, I will then give you one thousand dollars." "I am
old enough to make that bargain now," said young Farragut. "I will accept the offer." The bargain was closed,
and when young Farragut was twenty-one the cash was
handed over to him. A smoking boy can save a thousand
dollars in a few years in the same way, besides saving
physical energy and moral power.—*Popular Educator*

Birthday: Richard M. Milnes [Baron Houghton], an
English statesman and poet, born in London, England,
June 19, 1809; died at Vichy, France, Aug. 11 1885.

20 PUNCTUALITY

Time is always on the wing,
You can never stop its flight,
Then do at once your little task,
Happier you will be at night.

PUNCTUALITY

WHEN Washington's secretary excused himself for the
lateness of his attendance and laid the blame upon his
watch, his master quietly said, "Then you must get another
watch, or I another secretary." It will generally be found
that the men who are thus habitually behind time are

habitually behind success; and the world casts them aside
to swell the ranks of the grumblers and the railers against
fortune.

21 GENTLENESS

Every gentle word you say
One dark spirit drives away;

.   .   .   .

Every gentle deed you do
One bright spirit brings to you.
—*Virginia B. Harrison*

22 ADVERSITY

By adversity are wrought
The greatest works of admiration,
And all the fair examples of renown
Out of distress and misery are grown.

23 MANNERS

To be polite is to do and say
The kindest thing in the kindest way.

A GENTLEMAN

I KNEW him for a gentleman
  By signs that never fail:
His coat was rough and rather worn,
  His cheeks were thin and pale,—
A lad who had his way to make,
  With little time to play.
I knew him for a gentleman
  By certain signs to-day.

He met his mother on the street;
  Off came his little cap.
My door was shut; he waited there
  Until I heard his rap.

He took the bundle from my hand;
  And when I dropped my pen,
He sprang to pick it up for me,
  This gentleman of ten.

He does not push or crowd along;
  His voice is gently pitched;
He does not fling his books about
  As if he were bewitched.
He stands aside to let you pass;
  He always shuts the door;
He runs on errands willingly,
  To forge and mill and store.

He thinks of you before himself;
  He serves you if he can,
For in whatever company,
  The manners make the man;
At ten and forty 'tis the same,—
  The manner tells the tale,
And I discern the gentleman
  By signs that never fail.

24 IDLENESS

If you are idle, you are on the road to ruin, and
there are few stopping places upon it.—*H. W. Beecher*

Birthday: Henry Ward Beecher, a noted American
preacher, lecturer and writer, born in Litchfield, Conn.,
June 24, 1813; died in Brooklyn, N. Y., March 8, 1887.
(Son of Dr. Lyman Beecher and a brother of Harriet
Beecher Stowe.)

25 DUTY

Do whate'er you have to do
  With a true and earnest zeal;
Bend your sinews to the task;
  "Put your shoulders to the wheel."

THE DESERTED CHICKS

BY WILLIAM NORRIS BURR

THERE were six coops out in the chicken yard, each with a clucking mother hen inside, caring for her brood of chicks in mother-hen fashion.

Frank's father had given him the little Brown Leghorn family to care for. He was to give them their cornmeal at certain times every day and keep water in the pan, and once in a while let them out for a stroll over the little grass plot, where they could pick the green food that all chickens enjoy for a "relish."

One morning Frank's father came in with a very sober look on his face.

"Frank," said he, "how would you like to have father and mother go off to Los Angeles or somewhere to live and leave you here to take care of yourself?"

"Who'd get dinner, and—and—who'd drive the big grays?" asked Frank.

"Oh, I don't know," replied his father. "You would have to get your own dinner, I suppose, and just take care of yourself somehow."

"You—you're not going to do it, are you?" A lump had come into Frank's throat and it was not easy for him to talk.

"Don't you think it might help you to remember to do all your little chores?" asked Frank's father. "Who forgot last night to see that the brown hen and her chicks were snug?"

Frank hung his head and looked hard at the floor.

"I was playing with Eddie Ferris and—I guess I forgot," he said; and the lump almost choked him.

"And because Frank 'forgot,' the brown mother hen took the opportunity to go somewhere else to spend the night and left her chicks to take care of themselves; and the chicks are such tender little things that—well, they must have caught cold and some of them must have died."

"Did any of them die?" asked Frank.

"No," said his father, and there was a faint little twinkle in his eyes. "I happened to go through the chicken yard last night after dark and I discovered that the brown hen had deserted her brood, and what do you think I did for them?"

"I guess you hunted up their mother and told her she ought to stay at home with her children," answered Frank.

"No, it was too late then to be hunting up a runaway hen," smiled Frank's father, "so I got an old feather duster that is in pretty good condition yet, but has been used in the buggy shed and is not very clean, and I unscrewed the handle and gave those poor little deserted chicks that duster as a substitute for their mother. And they got through the night very comfortably, cuddled under the feathers of that duster. But they might have had their mother, who is their natural protector, if Frank had not forgotten to see if they were all right, at least by sundown."

"I don't want you and mother to go off to Los Angeles and leave me here," whispered Frank, and the lump came into his throat again. "There wouldn't be any one around to 'feather-duster' me."

"All right, my boy," said his father, heartily. "You'll not forget your chicks again, will you?"

"I'll try hard not to," promised Frank.

—*Sunday School Times*

26 NATURE

Open the door, let in the air;
The winds are sweet and the flowers are fair.

GREEN THINGS GROWING

BY DINAH MULOCK CRAIK

O THE green things growing, the green things growing,
The faint sweet smell of the green things growing!

I should like to live, whether I smile or grieve,
Just to watch the happy life of my green things growing.

O the fluttering and the pattering of those green things
  growing!
How they talk each to each, when none of us are knowing;
In the wonderful light of the weird moonlight
Or the dim, dreamy dawn when the cocks are crowing.

I love, I love them so—my green things growing!
And I think that they love me, without false showing;
For by many a tender touch, they comfort me so much,
With the soft mute comfort of green things growing.

27   FORBEARANCE

> Lift up your burden; it is God's gift, therefore bear
> it nobly.—*Helen Keller*

A JUNE MORNING LESSON

BY JULIA M. DANA

Twice one are two
Prairie roses, brushing through
My window, all cool with dew.
Twice one are two.

Twice two are four
Bees a humming round the door—
Calling others by the score.
Twice two are four.

Twice three are six
Pansy beds their colors mix;
See the mother hen and chicks—
Twice three are six.

Twice four are eight;
Gorgeous butterflies elate,
Dancing, poising, delicate,
Twice four are eight.

Twice five are ten
Sweetest strains from yonder glen,
Echoed o'er and o'er again,
Twice five are ten.

Twice six are twelve
Merry maidens of the year—
Some in snowy gowns appear,
Some in gold and silver sheer,
Yet the fairest is, I ween,
Dainty June in pink and green.

Read: Helen Keller's *Story of My Life.*
Sing: "Summer Time," from *Merry Melodies;* "The Summer Time," from Kellogg's *Best Primary Songs.*
Birthday: Helen A. Keller, an American author, born at Tuscumbia, Ala., June 27, 1880; lives in Wrentham, Mass.   Though deaf, dumb and blind from illness in infancy, she was enabled to study through the efforts of her teacher, Miss Anne M. Sullivan, and was graduated at Radcliffe College, Cambridge, Mass., in 1904.

28 HAPPINESS

Learn something beautiful, see something beautiful,
do something beautiful each day of your life.
—*Alice Freeman Palmer's "Three Rules of Happiness"*

Sing: "June," from Hanson's *Gems of Song.*
Birthday: Jean Jacques Rousseau, a French author, born in Geneva, Switzerland, June 28, 1712; died in Paris, France, July 2, 1778.

29 GRADUATION

And what is so rare as a day in June?
Then, if ever, come perfect days;
Then Heaven tries earth if it be in tune,
And over it softly her warm ear lays.
—*Lowell*

GRADUATION'S PROMISE

BY SALENA SHEETS MARTIN

'AND once again life opens wide the door
Through which shall pass ambition, youth and hope,
Into that harsher world, but little tried,
Where eager faith its tasks would meet and cope,
The tasks that stagger oft when youth seems far
From that fond hope that fastened to the star.

How fine a thing it is—this hope of youth,
Which bears the faithful heart that gives it room
Above all trivial things of time and place
On pinions to a sure success—not doom;
That sees no failures in the coming years
Whose eager feet press on—they know no fears.

The June time brings these fruitful days of life,
Repeating for each one the promise o'er,
Of rich fulfillment—harvests in the years,
The fields of time, in which our visions soar;
With roses to bloom and thorns but few,
May every worthy dream of youth come true.

And may no idle dreams usurp the mind,
No selfish visions stretch adown the years,
No loitering by waysides, seeming joy
To end in grief and penitential tears;
But on life's journey all along the way
Look Heavenward and for its guidance pray.

Sing: "Glad Vacation," from Hanson's *Silvery Notes.*

Birthdays: Peter Paul Rubens, a famous Flemish painter, born at Siegen, Germany, June 29, 1577; died at Antwerp, Belgium, May 30, 1640.

John Quincy Adams Ward, an American sculptor, born in Urbana, Ohio, June 29, 1830; died in New York City, May 1, 1910.

Celia Thaxter, an American writer, born in Portsmouth, N. H., June 29, 1836; died August 27, 1894.

John Bach MacMaster, an American historian, born in Brooklyn, N. Y., June 29, 1852.

30 VACATION

"Vacation is the time for fun!"
All girls and boys are saying
When schools and books grow wearisome,
And hearts are ripe for playing.
—*Mary D. Brine*

VACATION-TIME

ALL the world is set to rhyme
Now it is vacation-time,
And a swelling flood of joy
Brims the heart of every boy.
No more rote and no more rule,
No more staying after school
When the dreamy brain forgets
Tiresome tasks the master sets;
Nothing but to play and play
Through an endless holiday.

Morn or afternoon, may all
Swing the bat and catch the ball;
Nimble-footed, race and run
Through the meadows in the sun,
Chasing winged scraps of light,

Butterflies in darting flight;
Or where willows lean and look
Down at others in the brook,
Frolic loud the stream within,
Every arm a splashing fin.

Where the thorny thickets bar,
There the sweetest berries are;
Where the shady banks make dim
Pebbly pools, shy trout swim;
Where the boughs are mossiest,
Builds the humming-bird a nest;—
There are haunts the rover seeks,
Touch of tan upon his cheeks,
And within his heart the joy
Known to no one but a boy.

All the world is set to rhyme
Now it is vacation-time.
                    —*From "Book of Rhyme"*

Sing: "Vacation's Coming" and "Vacation Song," from *School Song Knapsack.*

INDEX

LIST OF REFERENCE BOOKS

Frequently mentioned in MORNING EXERCISES FOR ALL THE YEAR and which will be sent postpaid at the following prices by the publishers of this book:

		Price
Alice's Adventures in Wonderland—*Carroll*	Cloth	$0.35
American Book of Golden Deeds—*Baldwin*	Cloth	.50
American Inventions and Inventors—*Mowry*	Cloth	.65
American School Songs	Muslin	.20
Best Christmas Book, The—*Sindelar*	Paper	.30
Best Primary Songs—*Kellogg*	Paper	.15
Boston Collection of Kindergarten Stories	Cloth	.60
Can You Believe Me Stories—*Aspinwall*	Cloth	1.50
Cat-Tails and Other Tales—*Howliston*	Cloth	.40
Child's Christ Tales—*Proudfoot*	Cloth	.75
Child's Garden of Verses, A—*Stevenson*	Cloth	.40
Child's Song Book—*Howliston*	Boards	.30
Ethics for Children—*Cabot*	Cloth	1.25
Fables and Folk Stories—*Scudder*	Cloth	.45
Fairy Stories and Fables—*Baldwin*	Cloth	.35
Fifty Famous Stories Retold—*Baldwin*	Cloth	.35
For the Children's Hour—*Bailey and Lewis*	Cloth	1.50
Gems of Song—*Hanson*	Boards	.35
Golden Windows, The—*Richards*	Cloth	1.00
Household Stories—*Klingensmith*	Cloth	.35
How to Celebrate Arbor Day—*Kellogg*	Paper	.25
How to Tell Stories to Children—*Bryant*	Cloth	1.00
In the Child's World—*Poulsson*	Cloth	2.00
Just-So Stories—*Kipling*	Cloth	1.50
Kindergarten Stories and Morning Talks—*Wiltse*	Cloth	.75
Language Through Nature, Literature and Art—*Allison and Purdue*	Cloth	.45
Lincoln Day Entertainments—*Sindelar*	Paper	.25
Merry Melodies—*Hanson*	Paper	.15
May Intermediate Plan Book—*George*	Paper	.25
More Five Minute Stories—*Richards*	Cloth	1.00
Mother Stories—*Lindsay*	Cloth	1.00
Nature Myths and Stories—*Cooke*	Cloth	.35
Nixie Bunny in Manners-Land—*Sindelar*	Cloth	.40
October Primary Plan Book—*George*	Paper	.25
Our Holidays: Retold from St. Nicholas	Cloth	.75
Perfect Tribute, The—*Andrews*	Boards	.50
Pig Brother, The—*Andrews*	Cloth	1.00
Robert Louis Stevenson Songs—*Crowninshield*	Boards	.60
School Song Knapsack—*Pattengill*	Paper	.10
Silvery Notes—*Hanson*	Paper	.15
Songs Every One Should Know—*Johnson*	Cloth	.50
Songs in Season—*George*	Paper	.50
Stories from Life—*Marden*	Cloth	.45
Stories from Plato—*Burt*	Cloth	.40
Stories of Useful Inventions—*Forman*	Cloth	.60
Story Hour, The—*Wiggin and Smith*	Cloth	1.00
Story of My Life—*Helen Keller*	Cloth	1.50
Story-tell Lib—*Slosson*	Cloth	.50
Thanksgiving Entertainments—*Sindelar*	Paper	.25
Thirty More Famous Stories Retold—*Baldwin*	Cloth	.50
True Bird Stories—*Miller*	Cloth	.60
True Fairy Stories—*Bakewell*	Cloth	.35
Uncle Sam's School Songs—*Langley, Martin and Towne*	Muslin	.20
Washington Day Entertainments—*Sindelar*	Paper	.30
White's School Management	Cloth	1.00

THE PROGRESSIVE SCHOOL CLASSICS

For Supplementary Reading and Study

A NEW series of reading books, which offers the highest class of literature for all grades, designed to supplement or replace the regular reading books. This is the only series of complete classics from standard authors at so low a price that contains all of the following features:

Accurate and authentic texts—Notes and numbered lines for reference—Portraits, biographical sketches, and illustrations—New, clean type, graded in size according to the age of the child—Good grade of school-book paper, neat and durable binding—Uniform and convenient size.

The grading here given conforms to that adopted by a majority of schools. However, after each title, we indicate the range of grades within which the book may be read with satisfactory results. The following titles have been published. Others are in preparation.

Price, per copy, 5 cents, postpaid, unless otherwise mentioned.

SECOND YEAR

Bow-Wow and Mew-Mew. Grades 1-3. By Georgiana M. Craik. Edited by Joseph C. Sindelar. The story of a young dog and cat. **Price, 12 cents.**

FIFTH YEAR

The King of the Golden River. Grades 4-6. By John Ruskin. 32 pages.

SIXTH YEAR

Rip Van Winkle and The Author's Account of Himself. Grades 5-8. By Washington Irving. From *The Sketch Book*. 32 pages.

The Legend of Sleepy Hollow. Grades 5-8. By Washington Irving. From *The Sketch Book*. 32 pages.

Thanatopsis and Other Poems. Grades 5-8. By William Cullen Bryant. In addition to the title poem, the book contains a choice selection of Bryant's best-known poems. 32 pages.

SEVENTH YEAR

The Courtship of Miles Standish. Grades 6-8. By Henry W. Longfellow. The complete poem in good type, with notes, biographical sketch, portrait, and numbered lines. 40 pages.

Evangeline. Grades 6-8. By Henry W. Longfellow. The complete poem, uniform in style with *Miles Standish*. 48 pages.

The Great Stone Face. Grades 6-8. By Nathaniel Hawthorne. One of Hawthorne's best sketches from *Twice-Told Tales*. 32 pages.

The Man Without a Country. Grades 6-8. By Edward Everett Hale. The complete text of Dr. Hale's best and incomparable story, printed in good type, with notes, a biographical sketch, portrait, numbered lines. 32 pages.

Snow-Bound and Other Poems. Grades 6-8. By John G. Whittier. In addition to this winter idyll, the book includes his The Corn Song and The Barefoot Boy. 32 pages.

EIGHTH YEAR

Enoch Arden. Grades 6-8. By Alfred Tennyson. 32 pages.

The Vision of Sir Launfal and Other Poems. Grades 6-8. By James Russell Lowell. 32 pages.

BECKLEY-CARDY CO.   **Educational Publishers**   **CHICAGO**

THE NIXIE BUNNY BOOKS

—By Joseph C. Sindelar—

NIXIE BUNNY IN MANNERS-LAND

A Rabbit Story of Good Manners

It CAN truthfully be said that very few children's books have enjoyed anything equal to the great popularity of the Nixie Bunny series. From the very first day of publication the success of NIXIE BUNNY IN MANNERS-LAND has been phenomenal. It is a rabbit fairy story of good manners, and a volume which has been found a welcome guest into the realm of animal story books. It is seldom that one finds a story which so incorporates the proper training along with higher thought, education, and a style which so captures the children's interest. The book is full of fun and fancy, and is so attractive that even babies like it for its bunny pictures. It has been read by over 50,000 children in two years, and is used widely as a supplementary reader in the second and third grades.

The *Chicago Evening Post* says of NIXIE BUNNY IN MANNERS-LAND: "Among books which are made only to sell, this one stands out by virtue of its difference. It is made to read, and the children will enjoy and profit by it."

With 64 illustrations in colors and decorated end papers

144 pages. Cloth binding, stamped in two colors

Price, 40 cents

NIXIE BUNNY IN WORKADAY-LAND

A Rabbit Story of the Occupations

A COMPANION volume to NIXIE BUNNY IN MANNERS-LAND, and a book which alone can rival it in popularity. It is written in the same choice and delightful style, and has been designed to supply the little folks with a reader of occupation and industry in the form of a fairy tale.

Henry Turner Bailey, Editor of *School-Arts Magazine*, and a noted art critic, says: "NIXIE BUNNY IN WORKADAY-LAND, by Joseph C. Sindelar, with illustrations by Helen Geraldine Hodge, is the successor of that success, NIXIE BUNNY IN MANNERS-LAND. The love of children for these rabbits is one of the wonders of the pedagogical world!"

With 90 illustrations in colors and decorated end papers

144 pages. Cloth binding, stamped in two colors

Price, 40 cents

The Nixie Bunny books have been adopted by fourteen States, by Chicago, Pittsburgh, Rochester, Worcester (Mass.), and hundreds of towns and cities all over the country, and are cherished by children everywhere.

Specimen pages mailed free upon request

BECKLEY-CARDY CO.   **Educational Publishers**   **CHICAGO**

MORNING EXERCISES FOR ALL THE YEAR
─────A DAY BOOK FOR TEACHERS─────

By Joseph C. Sindelar
Author of Nixie Bunny in Manners-Land,
Nixie Bunny in Workaday-Land, etc.

THIS is a new work—just published—and the only really complete and systematic book of opening exercises that has yet been issued. It contains over 300 exercises, arranged day by day, there being an exercise for each morning of the ten school months, beginning with the first day in September and ending with the last day in June. There is an appropriate literary quotation for each day—303 in all, 100 interesting stories, anecdotes and recreations, a goodly number of poems, many birthday exercises and those of the seasons, special day programs, related songs and readings, Bible references, etc. The exercises are in endless variety, emphasizing moral principles and teaching lessons of proper conduct, right thought, ideals of life, and the appreciation of nature, literature, science, and art. Each day has its own lesson and an abundance of the best material for use therewith. All special days and school occasions, also birthdays of noted men and women, are duly recorded and suitably commemorated. The material is for all grades, and the teacher will find the book an invaluable aid in her work.

224 pages. Cloth. Price, 60 cents

THE BEST CHRISTMAS BOOK
Edited by Joseph C. Sindelar

THERE is nothing better or newer published in the way of Christmas entertainments. The material contained in this book is fresh and original, much of it having been written specially by Marie Irish, Harriette Wilbur, and Thos. B. Weaver. There is a wealth of new ideas, and a complete program for everyone. It is positively the "Best" book of Christmas entertainment exercises published. Arranged according to grades.

The following list of classified contents will show the variety and scope of the work. Contents: 82 recitations, 36 quotations, 4 monologues and readings, 10 dialogues, exercises and plays, 7 fancy drills and marches, 4 acrostics and motion songs, 3 tableaux, 4 pantomimes and pantomimed songs, 9 songs with music, 8 songs of new words to old tunes, 14 facts regarding Christmas and Christmas customs in other lands.

Illustrated. 192 pages. Paper. Price, 30 cents

BECKLEY-CARDY CO.   **Educational Publishers**   **CHICAGO**

CPSIA information can be obtained
at www.ICGtesting.com
Printed in the USA
BVHW041053170620
581539BV00007B/737